STRATEGY
BITES
BACK

STRATEGY BITES BACK

IT IS A LOT MORE, AND LESS, THAN YOU EVER IMAGINED ....

HENRY MINTZBERG
BRUCE AHLSTRAND
JOSEPH LAMPEL

PEARSON PRENTICE HALL
AN IMPRINT OF PEARSON EDUCATION
Upper Saddle River, NJ • Boston • Indianapolis • New York • London
San Francisco • Toronto • Sydney • Tokyo • Singapore • Hong Kong •
Cape Town • Madrid • Paris • Milan • Munich • Amsterdam
www.ft-ph.com

Library of Congress Catalog Number: 2004117139

Publisher: Tim Moore
Acquisitions Editor: Paula Sinnott
Editorial Assistant: Richard Winkler
Marketing Manager: Martin Litkowski
International Marketing Manager: Tim Galligan
Cover Designer: Chuti Prasertsith
Managing Editor: Gina Kanouse
Senior Project Editor: San Dee Phillips
Copy Editor: Keith Cline
Proofreader: Kayla Dugger
Senior Indexer: Cheryl Lenser
Compositor: Jake McFarland
Manufacturing Buyer: Dan Uhrig

Prentice Hall offers excellent discounts on this book when ordered in
quantity for bulk purchases or special sales. For more information, please
contact U.S. Corporate and Government Sales, 1-800-382-3419, corpsales@
pearsontechgroup.com. For sales outside the U.S., please contact International
Sales, international@pearsontechgroup.com.

Printed in the United States of America
First Printing February, 2005
ISBN 0-13-185777-0

Pearson Education LTD.
Pearson Education Australia PTY, Limited.
Pearson Education Singapore, Pte. Ltd.
Pearson Education North Asia, Ltd.
Pearson Education Canada, Ltd.
Pearson Educatión de Mexico, S.A. de C.V.
Pearson Education—Japan
Pearson Education Malaysia, Pte. Ltd.

ACKNOWLEDGMENTS

The publishers are grateful to the following companies and individuals for permission to reproduce copyright material:

The Financial Times (pp. 15, 23, 268) © Financial Times 2003, 2004; Eenie, meenie, minie, mo (p. 19) © The Economist Newspaper Limited, London, 20 March; Five ps for Strategy (p. 26) ©1987, by The Regents of the University of California. Reprinted from the California Management Review, Vol 30, No. 1. By permission of the Regents; Beware of Strategy (p.29) The Seeking of Strategy Where It Is Not: Toward a Theory of Strategy Absense, A. Inkpen and N. Choudbury, © 1995, John Wiley & Sons Limited. Reproduced with permission; Next (p. 30) ©1984, by The Regents of the University of California. Reprinted from the California Management Review, Vol 30, No. 1. By permission of the Regents; The CEO as Strategist (p. 43) By Keith Hammonds, © 2004 Gruner + Jahr USA Publishing. First published in *Fast Company* Magazine. Reprinted with permissions; The Tortoise and The Hare (p. 46) ´John Kay; The Seven Deadly Sins of Planning (p. 62) Reprinted from Long Range Planning, Vol 27, Ian Wilson, Strategic Planning Isn't Dead—It Changed, pp. 12–24., ©1994 with permission from Elsevier; How To Plan A Strategy (p. 74) Reprinted with the permission of The Free Press, a Division of Simon & Schuster Adult Publishing Group, from TOP MANAGEMENT PLANNING by George A Steiner. Copyright © 1969 by George A Steiners. All rights reserved; Management and Magic (p. 87) ©1984, by The Regents of the University of California. Reprinted from the California Management Review, Vol 27, No. 3. By permission of the Regents; Positioning the Derrière: Toilet Nirvana (p. 111) Copyright © 2002 by the New York Times Co. Reprinted with permission; Reversing the Images of BCG's Growth/Share Matrix (p. 120) Strategic Management Journal, John Seeger, 1984, John Wiley & Sons Ltd. Reproduced by permission of John Wiley & Sons Limited; Entreprenurship and Planning (p. 146) Reprinted by permission of Harvard Business Review from The Entrepreneur's Craft Strategies that Work by Amar Bhide, March–April 1994. Copyright © by the Harvard Business School Publishing Corporation; all rights reserved; Biases and Limitations of Judgment: Humans (p. 162) Reprinted and edited with the permission of The Free Press, a Division of Simon & Schuster Adult Publishing Group, from FORECASTING, PLANNING AND STRATEGY FOR THE 21st CENTURY by Spyros G. Makkridakis. Copyright © 1990 by Spyros G. Makridakis. All rights reserved; Everything I Need to Know about Strategy I Learned at the National Zoo (p. 167) *The Journal of Business Strategy* (Emerald Group Publishing Ltd) Vol 18, 1, January/February, 1997; pp. 8–11; The Man vs the Machine (p. 175) Copyrighted 2003, Chicago Tribune Company. All rights reserved. Used with permission; Think Like a Grandmaster (p. 178) Chrysalis Books [Kotov 1971, BT Batsford: London]; Management Expert Gary Hamel talks with Enron's Ken Lay about what it's like to launch a new strategy in the Real World (p. 183) FORTUNE, Gary Hamel © 1997 Time Inc. All rights reserved; Good Managers Don't Make Policy Decisions (p. 190) Reprinted by permission of Harvard Business Review from Good Managers don't make policy decisions by H. Edward Wrapp, Sept–Oct 1967. Copyright © by the Harvard Business School Publishing Corporation; all rights reserved; From the interview with Honda Managers (p. 201) ©1984, by The Regents of the University of California. Reprinted from the California Management Review, Vol 27, No. 1. By permission of the Regents; Strategies That Learn (p. 212) FORTUNE, Gary Hamel © 1997 Time Inc. All rights reserved; Top-down transformation (p.218) Reprinted by permission of Harvard Business Review from Leading Change: why transformation efforts fail by J.P. Kotter, March–April 1995. Copyright © by the Harvard Business School Publishing Corporation; all rights reserved; Bottom-up change (p. 219) Reprinted by permission of Harvard Business Review from Why change programs don't produce change by Michael Beer, R A Eisenstat, B Spector, Nov–Dec 1990. Copyright © by the Harvard Business School Publishing Corporation; all rights reserved; Laws of Power (p. 237) From THE 40 LAWS OF POWERS by Robert Greene and Joost Elffers, ©1998 by Robvert Greene and Joost Elffers. Used by permission of Viking Penguin, a division of Penguin Group (USA) Inc; Strategy is Culture is Strategy (p. 257) Karl E Weick, The Significance of Corporate Culture in Peter J Frost et al., *Organisational Culture*, pp. 381–389, copyright 1985 by Sage Publications. Reprinted by permissions of Sage Publications, Inc.

CONTENTS

CHAPTER 3
STRATEGY CAREFULLY

CHAPTER 4
FIGURING STRATEGY

CHAPTER 5
A VISION OF STRATEGY

CHAPTER 6
INSIDE THE STRATEGIST'S HEAD

CHAPTER 7
STRATEGY A STEP AT A TIME

CHAPTER 8
STRATEGY WITH THE GLOVES OFF AND THE HALO ON

CHAPTER 9
FINAL FOOD FOR THOUGHT

STRATEGY FOR FUN

Strategy can be awfully boring. The consultants can be straighter than we academics, not to mention the planners. Everybody is so serious. If that gets us better strategies, fine. But it often gets us worse ones—standard, generic, uninspiring. Strategy doesn't only have to position, it also has to inspire. So an uninspiring strategy is really no strategy at all.

The most interesting companies we know, often the most successful, are not boring. They have novel, creative, inspiring, sometimes even playful strategies. By taking the whole strategy business less seriously, they end up with more serious results—and have some fun in the bargain.

So this book has a serious intention; to take strategy less seriously and so promote better strategies. Besides, why not have a good time reading a strategy book for a change? Isn't it time for strategy to bite back?

The three of us teamed up earlier to do a serious book on strategy, albeit with a not-so-serious title: *Strategy Safari*. We played with that title here and there, but mostly we set out to order and review the serious literature about strategy. We think we did a good job and recommend that book to you. It was written for your head—now here comes one for your heart. As you may have noticed, heads and hearts go together. So this book fills the gap in a field with so much head.

We organized *Strategy Safari* around ten schools of thought, from planning to positioning, visionary to venturing, etc. We use a similar structure here but with seven views, renamed and lightened up. But that is where these two books part company. For here we don't so much offer straight description as images, impressions, insights. Most books *say* it. If you read the words, they assume you *got* it. The trouble is you can just as quickly *lose* it. So here we set out, whenever possible, to *show* it so that you can *see* it. Then you'll never *forget* it.

We call this collection *bytes* because we searched for really interesting excerpts on strategy, as short as we could find, or make, them. We wanted each to have a maximum of three pages. Most, but not all, do. You will find some classic material among these bytes, drawn from key sources, supplemented with stories of strategy in action, often with an unusual twist. But mostly this book contains all kinds of wild and wooly things—poems, quotations, cartoons . . . whatever we could find on paper that enlightens about strategy. We did not want nutty stuff, at least for its own sake, but eye-opening stuff, which can sometimes appear nutty. Bear in mind that many of the great strategies of this world initially appeared nutty too.

We also call some of these readings *bites* because we have felt no obligation to always be polite about all this. We did not look for criticism for its own sake, but neither have we shied away from critical material that provides insight. Entrenched beliefs that have outlived their usefulness sometimes have to be challenged by a good push. And strategy certainly is a field full of such beliefs. One of our beliefs, in contrast, is that there are no prophets in this field. There are certainly people worth paying attention to, and we give many of them space in this book, but none is a prophet because all views are vulnerable. Only when you, as a reader, put them together—see them in juxtaposition and combine them in application—do they come usefully alive. As Gary Hamel put it, starkly, "The dirty little secret of the strategy industry is that it doesn't have any theory of strategy creation." Strategy has to come out of a creative process conducted by thoughtful people. Profits and prophets don't mix well in strategy.

We summarize below the various views that make up the main chapters of this book, sandwiched between a first one to get you going, on that word "strategy," and a last one to ease you back into the real world of shareholder value and other easy answers.

SWOTed by strategy

We begin with the most established view of strategy, epitomized by the conductor up on the podium—a favored metaphor, in fact. Here, the chief pronounces strategy from on high so that everyone else can scurry around "implementing" it.

Key to this view is achieving a fit between internal Strengths and Weaknesses and external Opportunities and Threats—hence the SWOT model. It has much to recommend it, as you will see in some of the bytes, and lots to be critical about too, as you will see in the bites. After all, the conductor has rehearsals too, and they do not always go quite so smoothly as the concert. Besides, who is the real strategist—the conductor or the composer?

Strategy carefully

Open your newspaper and turn to the horoscope. (Maybe you do already but don't tell anybody.) There your future is neatly laid out for you. This second view of strategy is curiously similar. It proceeds on the basis that the future can be laid out for organizations. It's called *strategic planning* and has been all the rage among American corporations and communist governments; they both like to control things. Of course, strategic planning is surrounded by all sorts of fancy paraphernalia: checklists, techniques, systems galore. But when you think about it, so too is astrology. (One of the bites lets you so think about it.)

OK, enough of the bite. Strategic planning is a serious business. The readings suggest why. They also suggest that strategic planning does not create strategies so much as plan out the consequences of strategies already created. That, too, is a serious business.

Figuring strategy

Here the strategist metamorphoses one step further, from the chief of SWOT and the planner of planning to the analyst of positioning.

Michael Porter of the Harvard Business School gave this view its great impetus, following on some earlier work by consulting firms, itself preceded by two millennia of theorizing about military strategy.

Here strategy reduces to a generic position selected through systematic analysis: Under condition x, you had better do y. So the job of the strategist is not to create new strategies so much as select the best of proven ones. Consultants and academics love this because it allows them to sink their teeth into some good "hard data" and promote their "scientific" truths. But has it been good for companies? Read on.

A vision of strategy

Moses came down from the mountain with "the word" on the tablets, only to discover everyone else worshipping the Golden Calf. Visionaries have had similar problems ever since. The great leaders appear with their great messages while the rest of us want to get on with our narrow prejudices.

The visionary—in business often the entrepreneur, but sometimes also niche players and turnaround artists in established organizations—sees beyond the designs, plans, and positions of the earlier views, to strategy as perspective—a unique worldview. As a consequence, out goes systematic planning and careful figuring and in comes inspiration, insight, and intuition in the leader's head.

Conventional consultants, planners, and academics are not amused: It leaves them little room to maneuver. And that, in turn, gave us great room to maneuver. The stories of the visionaries are wonderful; what a rich choice we had! But be careful; great stories can be dangerous ones, sometimes a little too enticing.

Inside the strategist's head

Wouldn't it be nice to know what goes on inside the head of someone making strategy? Some researchers—mostly cognitive, psychologists so-called—worry about that. Think of the tantalizing questions: How does the brain come up with a new idea? How do we process information? How do we put these together into strategies? Indeed, what form does strategy take in the brain: a model? a frame? a map? Unfortunately, the researchers have not gotten very far yet—these processes remain mysterious—but far enough to provide us with some interesting ideas.

Most of these are about pathologies. There is no shortage of distortion in our cognitive processes, and there is no shortage of academic researchers who take great glee in exposing it: how we misread information, get carried away with our own actions, and so on.

But our human brains do some rather remarkable things too, like putting together extraordinary creative and integrated strategies (think of the whole system of an IKEA); happily, other researchers in the field recognize this. They see strategies as creative interpretations invented in the mind. To them, "environment" is not something given, to be analyzed out there, but something invented, to be constructed in here. So in Chapter 6, we juxtapose these two very different perspectives on strategic thinking.

Strategy a step at a time

Mao Tse Tung said that a long journey begins with a single step. Strategy can seem like *Mission Impossible*: Things are so complicated, so interconnected; where do you begin? The answer: with a single step. Do something, anything. Venture! As you proceed you will learn, and as you learn you will build. Great strategies grow out of little initiatives.

The implications are profound, not the least being that anyone can be a strategist. After all, anyone can take that first step; that is, have the initial idea. Who knows where the great strategy shall begin. So here too, you can imagine the fun we had picking the bytes and bites. The one-step-at-a-time approach opens strategy up to a whole world of learning.

Is this, then, the "word"? No, not any more than any of the other views. But it is certainly part of the words worth reading.

Strategy with the gloves off and the halo on
Next we turn to a kind of yin and yang of strategy: its dark side of politics—or is it the realistic side?—and its light side of culture—or is that heavy?

Power and politics certainly convey another slice of reality; strategy can be a nasty business. Competitors are out to crush you, and not always in polite economic ways. They can deceive and backstab too. But then again, you too are a competitor, not always merely responding to what they do to you. And then there are your colleagues in your own organization, who can be doing the same sort of thing, while you are all supposed to be creating common strategy. Aren't we all supposed to be in this together, developing our strategies for the common good? Why, then, doesn't everyone else listen to me?

So we have two views of strategy as power and politics. In one, people within the organization push each other around, so that if strategies appear at all it is through the give and take of bargaining, jockeying, infighting, and all the rest.

In the other, the whole organization pushes its weight around in the world, maneuvering itself into strategies that are often less economic than political.

Now, hold power up to a mirror and the reverse image you see is culture. Where one focuses on self-interest and fragmentation, the other reflects common interest and integration—strategy as a social process rooted in culture.

Culture became a big issue in the West after Japanese management was recognized in the 1980s. It became clear that strategic advantage also lay in difficult-to-imitate factors deeply rooted in the history and traditions of an organization. Like a fine tapestry, this view encourages an organization to weave its various beliefs and activities into a tight and unique strategy. But like a tapestry, that makes it difficult to take the strategy apart. If one part—one strand, one color, one product line—no longer works, you might have to throw the whole thing away and start over.

Japan may be having economic difficulties today, but the message of strategy rooted in culture remains as germane as it was in the 1980s. (Just ask people in the automobile business about the success of Toyota, a company that remains deeply rooted in the Japanese style of managing.) So the message of culture is ignored at your peril—and in this world of "shareholder value" it is being ignored a great deal. We put this as the last of our views because we believe it is time to bring it back to life.

So here you have it; seven views on a fascinating process. Will Rogers, the great American wit, once said, "I never met a man I did not like." We bet he did. But his point was that there is something likeable in everyone. So too there is something useful in each of these views on strategy—even, we are prepared to say with a little trepidation, some fun in each. So off we go.

This book is not particularly linear, so please do not feel obligated to read everything, or even, if you prefer, anything in any particular order. Do what suits you. Just enjoy it.

We have prepared some useful tools to help make your strategy sessions more incisive and to give your strategy more bite. You can find them at: www.pearson-books.com/StrategyBitesBack/.

F. Scott Fitzgerald reportedly said, "The test of a first-rate intelligence is the ability to hold two opposing ideas in the mind at the same time and still retain the ability to function." Here we offer you seven. Keep functioning! Have fun!

A final note to you, the reader.
We are thinking of two sequels:

Management Bites Back and *Organizations Bite Back*. So please send us the little gems, the bits and bytes and bites that you have come across. (You can send them to Bruce at bahlstrand@trentu.ca.)

CHAPTER 1
WHAT'S IN A WORD?

"Strategy is when you are out of ammunition, but keep on firing so that the enemy won't know."
(Anonymous)

"When in doubt, use a bigger hammer."
(Dobin's law)

"This is the course in advanced physics. That means the instructor finds the subject confusing. If he didn't, the course would be called elementary physics."
(Louis Alvarez, Nobel Laureate)

INTRODUCTION TO CHAPTER 1

What's in the word "strategy"? According to what
follows, a lot more, and a lot less, than you might
have imagined. Here, to start, we waste no time with
politeness and get right to it. The opening bite
reminds us about how empty the buzzwords of
management can be. The author, a prominent
columnist, does not mention strategy but you will get
the idea. Next is a byte from *The Economist* that
reviews strategy across several decades in several
pages; a quick summary of the field as it is. Then
another bite, by another prominent columnist and
economist, about what strategy is—tongue-in-cheek.
After this we get serious again—five straight
definitions of strategy all starting with *P*—before we
end with three views about why organizations should
not have strategies.

       If you think all of this is meant to confuse,
then you are right; it is called unfreezing, softening
you up for what follows. Welcome to the course in
Advanced Strategy!

WHAT'S IN A BUZZWORD?
BY LUCY KELLAWAY

What's in a word? Lucy Kellaway, who writes a
column for the *Financial Times*, found what's in
several of them by reading the annual report of a
prominent consulting firm. The field of strategy has
from time to time (1965–2005) been known to use
buzzwords too, not the least "strategy" itself. So heed
her words.

Last week I found myself on the Tube (London's subway system)
with nothing to read but Accenture's 2002 annual report. As the
London Underground barely functions at the moment, I had a
long time to study it and by the time I finally arrived at London
Bridge, I knew it as intimately as the passionate, world-class
people who wrote it.

     An annual report is meant to give a snapshot of a
company's finances at year end. This one also gives something
else, rarer and more useful: a linguistic snapshot of current
business usage. In just a few short pages it assembles the most
popular clichés, making it a valuable document that will allow
future generations to understand how the business world thought
and wrote as of December 31, 2002.

     For those who do not have a copy of Accenture's
report, or whose preferred Tube reading is about why Wacko Jacko
is a great dad, I have compiled a list of the most popular words and
phrases that no business writing should be without. What
interests me are not the clumsy bits of jargon such as "business

process outsourcing capabilities," which form the backbone of the report, but the normal words, fed to us over and over again, until we become desensitised, left with no idea of what they mean at all:

> **Deliver.** This verb is straight in at number one. If you think "delivery" is something that involves a truck, and which IKEA charges for, you are sadly out of date. Accenture delivers all manner of things, none of which requires a truck or even a bicycle. "Innovation Delivered," it says on the cover, which sounds splendid and is ambiguous enough to be unchallengeable.

  Inside, there are five *D*-words in one short paragraph. Under the heading "Global Strategic Delivery Approach," we learn that "the ultimate goal is to deliver price competitive solutions." This is done through "a global network of delivery centres," which "enhance the ability to deliver results." This sounds a bit circular—but maybe that's the point.

  There are also more advanced grammatical forms—deliverables, and delivering on something. The grocery van delivers on Tuesday; Accenture "delivers on great ideas."

> **Value.** The Accenture report shows there are 101 Ways With Value. You can unleash and unlock it (see below). You can create it. You can capture it. You can have a "value opportunity." And, of course, it is not safe to leave the house without a "value proposition" in your back pocket. Does "value" mean the same in all these cases? Is it so vague that it means nothing at all?

> **Solutions.** These are the new products and services. They are what we deliver. Last year I wrote an entire column on the solutions craze and this report is filled

with them. There are "scalable solutions," "solutions units," "outsourcing solutions," and "robust and repeatable solutions," to name just a very, very few.

> **To drive.** I drive a Ford Galaxy. Accenture does a lot of driving, too, but its driving doesn't involve wheels. Instead, it "drives" growth. Or new revenues. Or change. All this driving gives the impression that the entity behind the wheel is in control—which is almost bound not to be the case.

> **To leverage.** This noun-as-verb has been in the charts for a long time but still deserves a mention. "We have a long track record of success leveraging ... solutions." "We leverage our global scale." Also leveraged are assets and expertise. I think this verb means "to do," or "to make the most of" but I wouldn't swear to it.

> **To unleash.** "Unleashing" is what you do when you take your dog for a walk, and then it usually cocks its leg on something. But now "to unleash" is a useful verb that can be applied to almost any positive activity—creativity, value, and so on. And if you don't want to "unleash," you can "unlock" instead.

> **Unparalleled.** This golden oldie is as good as ever. It works nicely as follows: "Enabling us to deliver innovation at unparalleled speed." "Unparalleled speed" must mean faster than the speed of light—which really would be innovation delivered.

> **Track record.** Never say "record" without the word "track" in front of it and "proven," or "unparalleled" after it.

Once you have mastered the above you are ready for whole sentences. The Accenture report interlaces snappy short ones, preferably clichés, aphorisms, truisms, and so on, with meatier phrases. "There is no time like the present." Or "We live in turbulent times." Or "Why Accenture?" (Why, indeed?) And then, having lulled readers into thinking they are with you, you hit them with something like: "Outsourcing is charged with aggressively expanding our global network of delivery centres as well as what we call our 'solutions workforce' to help us lower our technology solutions costs." Phew!

As an English student, I was sometimes given a difficult Shakespeare passage to take apart phrase by phrase. I always found that when I had finished I liked it better and understood it more.

When I first glanced at the Accenture report on the Tube platform, I felt I had got the drift of it. But now I have broken it down into little bits, I have lost my confidence and can't say I understand a single word.

Source: Originally published with the title "Delivering on Clichés: Accenture's Annual Report Almost Makes Sense—Until You Read it Phrase by Phrase," *Financial Times*, February 17, 2003, London edition, p. 12.

"EENIE, MEENIE, MINIE, MO . . . ."
THE ECONOMIST

Hang on—*The Economist* is taking us on a tour of strategy over several decades in several pages. From the classics to the latest, *The Economist* is careful with its words.

Top managers of big firms devote the bulk of their efforts to formulating strategy, though there is remarkably little agreement about what this is.

No single subject has so dominated the attention of managers, consultants, and management theorists as the subject of corporate strategy. For the top managers of big companies, this is perhaps understandable. Served by hordes of underlings, their huge desks uncluttered by the daily minutiae of business, they often consider setting strategy as their most valuable contribution. And it is also understandable that there is a great deal of debate about which strategies work best; business is, after all, complicated and uncertain. More puzzling is the fact that the consultants and theorists jostling to advise businesses cannot even agree on the most basic of all questions: What, precisely, is a corporate strategy?

      In . . . [an article in] the *Harvard Business Review*, Gary Hamel and C. K. Prahalad, professors at the London Business School and the University of Michigan, turn much recent thinking upside down by asserting that the real function of a company's strategy is not to match its resources with its opportunities, as many businessmen assume, but rather to set goals which "stretch" a company beyond what most of its managers believe is possible . . . .

The authors' reduction of strategy to little more than a rallying cry is the apotheosis of a trend away from formal planning at big firms which has been gathering pace for the past 30 years. In a vast outpouring of writing on the subject during this period, management theorists have come up with so many alternative views of what a corporate strategy should contain that they have undermined the entire concept. A growing number of businessmen now question whether thinking consciously about an overall strategy is of any benefit at all to big firms. Grabbing opportunities or coping with blows as they arise may make more sense.

Soon after the Second World War, when a new class of professional managers began to search for ideas about how to run big firms, the original view of strategy was borrowed from the military. Managers still talk about "attacking" markets and "defeating" rivals, but the analogy between generalship and running a firm was quickly abandoned when businessmen realized that slaughtering your opponents and outselling them had little in common.

By the 1960s corporate strategy had come to mean a complex and meticulously wrought plan based on detailed forecasts of economies and specific markets. That view was endorsed by two celebrated books: Alfred Sloan's *My Years With General Motors*, a memoir by the man who made the car maker the world's biggest industrial enterprise; and Alfred Chandler's *Strategy and Structure*, a history of big, successful American firms in which the Harvard professor argued that their strategies had produced their multidivisional form.

This approach to strategy fell into disrepute for several reasons. Many people blame it for the overzealous diversification of the following decade and the creation of poorly performing conglomerates. In the 1970s the success of Japanese firms, which seemed to eschew detailed planning, cast further doubt on its usefulness. The two sudden oil-price rises of the 1970s also meant that many firms had to tear up their plans and start again. Most revealing of all, many companies found that the reams of statistics and targets, once assembled, sat gathering dust. Occupied with running their operations, few managers at any level of the firm ever bothered to refer again to its handsomely bound corporate strategy.

Few managers ever bothered to refer again to its handsomely bound corporate strategy.

Then, in 1980, came another book: *Competitive Strategy* by Michael Porter, an economist at Harvard Business School. He argued that a firm's profitability was determined by the characteristics of its industry and the firm's position within it, so these should also determine its strategy. Applying the analytical techniques common to industrial economics, Mr. Porter said that a firm's primary task was to find niches it could defend from competitors, either becoming the low-cost producer, differentiating its products in a way which would allow it to command a higher profit margin, or erecting barriers to the entry of new rivals. Mr. Porter's book was an instant hit.

Nonetheless, his ideas have had little impact on how most big firms go about formulating strategy. One reason is that Mr. Porter's work is descriptive/not prescriptive. His vast checklists provide little guide to what firms should actually do, or avoid doing. Every firm would like to be in an industry with high barriers to entry, weak rivals and high profits. But few are so lucky.

About the same time as Mr. Porter's book appeared, James Quinn, a professor at Dartmouth College's Amos Tuck

Business School, published the results of a study of how big firms actually went about formulating strategy. He found that they proceeded by trial and error, constantly revising their strategy in the light of new experience. He called this "logical incrementalism." To a lot of people this sounded suspiciously like "muddling through" (i.e., no strategy at all), though Mr. Quinn vehemently denied this, arguing that there were great benefits to formalizing the process.

The most influential strain of theorizing about strategy in the 1980s has stressed expanding a firm's skills—rapid product development, high-quality manufacturing, technological innovation and service—and then finding markets in which to exploit those skills. This argument was made by Messrs. Hamel and Prahalad themselves in a 1990 *Harvard Business Review* article.

Despite the changing fashions, decades of theorizing have not been entirely useless. How a company views strategy does depend largely on its circumstances. Small firms determined to challenge behemoths may find it helpful to call their aspirations a "strategy." Big companies defending a dominant market position may find Mr. Porter's industry analysis illuminating. All firms should try to exploit and hone their skills. But there is no single way to approach the future. The next time your boss proudly boasts that he is off to a strategic-planning meeting, give him your condolences.

Source: © *The Economist Newspaper Limited*, London (March 20, 1993).

WHAT IS STRATEGY?
BY JOHN KAY

Yin and yang. Back to yin—or is it yang? John Kay, respected columnist and reputable economist, has trouble with the strategy buzzwords too.

No self-respecting business today would be without a strategy. But what is a strategy? The modern student is often confused by the many different uses of the words strategy and strategic.

Probably the commonest sense in which the word strategy is used today is as a synonym for expensive. You can always be sure that this meaning is intended when the term strategy is used in a context which involves advice. Here are some examples of strategy meaning costly. "We are strategy consultants," "Can we help you with your strategy?" "I advise company x on its strategy." These can be interpreted respectively as "our fees are very high," "we hope to send you a large bill," and "company x pays me a lot of money." Another useful term is "strategy weekend," which means a lot of people eating good food and fine wine at a country house hotel.

"Strategy means expensive" is also the key to understanding phrases like "strategic investment" and "strategic acquisition." This is a "strategic investment" should be translated as "we are going to lose a lot of money on this project." "This is a strategic acquisition" means "we are paying more for this company than it is worth."

The word strategy is also often used to mean important. You can recognize this in the phrase "I'm in strategy," which means "I have a large office, large salary, and the ear of the chief executive." "An interesting proposal, but does it have strategic significance?" can be translated as "I am not going to waste my time with things like this." And when the accountants, the human resources department, and the public relations people explain how they need to be involved in the firm's strategic planning, what they are saying is that they don't receive enough attention.

This interpretation of the word strategy has crept into everyday usage. When I picked up a leaflet the other day which described an English language gospel ministry as a truly strategic enterprise, I think what they meant was that they were engaged in an important activity.

"Strategy means important" is closely related, but not identical to, another meaning of strategy. In this, strategy is what the chief executive does. Thus, "Mr. A deals with the strategic issues while Ms. B is concerned with operations" means "Mr. A has a much larger salary and many more share options than Ms. B." Importance is, of course, a relative concept, specific to the environment of the firm. What is important is, by definition, what the important people do. Running the business is not necessarily important.

This kind of usage is exemplified in another meaning of strategy: Strategy is about acquisitions and disposals. This interpretation is virtually universal in the City (the financial district of London). "We don't understand company x's strategy" means "we haven't heard about (or aren't hired for) any deals involving company x." "Firm y has no strategy" means it hasn't bought or sold any other companies recently. This concept is reflected in the common financial market term "corporate activity," which covers financial restructuring and acquisitions. The opposite of "corporate activity" is "corporate inactivity," which describes the rest of a company's operations—making things and encouraging customers to buy them . . . .

There is more vacuity about strategy than about any other topic in business today. (I wrote that down but I'm not sure I believe it—there is a lot of vacuity about.) But there is a real issue and a real

There is more vacuity about strategy than about any other topic in business today.

subject of strategy for the corporation. And because strategy is based on distinctive capabilities, there are no generic strategies. There really are many interpretations of strategy. Strategy is what is right for you.

Source: *Financial Times*, August 5, 1998.

FIVE Ps FOR STRATEGY
BY HENRY MINTZBERG

One of us tries to sort all this out. Seriously. Five different definitions of strategy; all begin with a *P*.

Strategy is a plan

To almost anyone you care to ask, *strategy is a plan*—some sort of *consciously intended* course of action, a guideline (or set of guidelines) to deal with a situation. A kid has a "strategy" to get over a fence, a corporation has one to capture a market. By this definition, strategies have two essential characteristics: They are developed *consciously and purposefully*.

Strategy is a ploy

As plan, a strategy can be a *ploy*, too, really just a specific "maneuver" intended to outwit an opponent or competitor. The kid may use the fence as a ploy to draw a bully into his yard, where his Doberman pincher awaits intruders. Likewise, a corporation may threaten to expand plant capacity to discourage a competitor from building a new plant. Here the real strategy (as plan, that is, the real intention) is the threat, not the expansion itself, and as such is a ploy.

Strategy is a pattern

But if strategies can be intended (whether as general plans or specific ploys), surely they can also be realized. In other words, defining strategy as a plan is not sufficient; we also need a definition that encompasses the resulting behavior. Thus a third definition is proposed: strategy is a *pattern*—specifically, *a pattern in a stream of actions*. By this definition, strategy is consistency in behavior, whether or not intended. To paraphrase Hume, strategies may result from human *actions* but not human designs. We can call this "emergent" strategy—where a pattern realized was not intended. Strategies, in other words, *form* as well as are *formulated*. So even good ones need not necessarily be conscious and purposeful.

Strategies may result from human *actions* but not human designs.

Strategy is a position

Strategy is also a *position*—specifically, a means of locating an organization in its "environment." In ecological terms, strategy becomes a "niche"; in management terms, a product-market "domain." Position is usefully identified with respect to competitors (literally so in the military, where position becomes the site of the battle).

Strategy is a perspective

While *position* looks out, seeking to locate the organization in the external environment, *perspective* looks inside the organization, indeed inside the heads of the strategists. Here, strategy becomes the ingrained way of perceiving the world. Some organizations, for example, are aggressive pacesetters, while others build protective shells around themselves. Strategy in this respect is to the organization what personality is to the individual.

Each of these definitions adds important elements to our understanding of strategy, indeed encourages us to address fundamental questions about organizations in general. As plan, strategy deals with how leaders try to establish direction for organizations, to set them on predetermined courses of action. As ploy, strategy takes us into the realm of direct competition, where threats and feints and other maneuvers are employed to gain advantage. This places the process of strategy formation in its most dynamic setting, with moves provoking countermoves and so on. As pattern, strategy focuses on action, reminding us that the concept is an empty one if it does not take behavior into account. As position, strategy encourages us to look at organizations in context, specifically in their competitive environments—how they decide on their products and markets and protect them in order to meet competition, avoid it, or subvert it. And finally as perspective, strategy raises intriguing questions about intention and behavior in a collective context.

Source: © 1987, by The Regents of the University of California. Adapted from the *California Management Review*, "The Strategy Concept 1: Five Ps for Strategy" by Henry Mintzberg, Vol 30, No 1. By permission of the Regents.

BEWARE OF STRATEGY
FIRST: BY A. INKPEN AND N. CHOUDHURY

Maybe strategy is not always such a good thing. So we suggest two different bytes.

> ... Strategy absence need not be associated with organizational failure ... Deliberate building-in of strategy absence may promote flexibility in an organization ... Organizations with tight controls, high reliance on formalized procedures, and a passion for consistency may lose the ability to experiment and innovate.

> Management may use the absence of strategy to send unequivocal signals to both internal and external stakeholders ... For example, various articles have described Nucor's disdain for formal planning systems and the firm's reliance instead on a consistency in action at all levels in the organization. Nucor has no written strategic plan, no written objectives, and no mission statement. For Nucor, an absence of many of the supposed elements of strategy is symbolic of the no-frills, nonbureaucratic organization Nucor has worked hard to become.

> An absence of a rigid pattern of strategic decision making may ensure that "noise" is retained in organizational systems, without which strategy may become a specialized recipe that decreases flexibility and blocks learning and adaptation ....

Source: Excerpted from "The Seeking of Strategy Where It Is Not: Toward a Theory of Strategy Absence" by A. Inkpen and N. Choudhury in *Strategic Management Journal* Vol. 16, 1995: pp. 313–323 © 1995, John Wiley & Sons Limited. Reproduced with permission.

NEXT: BY HENRY MINTZBERG

> Strategies are to organizations what blinders are to horses: They keep them going in a straight line, but impede the use of peripheral vision. By focusing effort and directing the attention of each part within the integrated whole, the organization runs the risk of being unable to change its strategy when it has to. Setting oneself on a predetermined course in unknown waters is the perfect way to sail straight into an iceberg. Sometimes it is better to move slowly, a little bit at a time, looking not too far ahead but very carefully, so that behavior can be shifted on a moment's notice. Besides, it is not always clear what a good strategy is, or indeed if it is not better at times to proceed without what amounts to the straitjacket of a clear intended strategy.

Strategies are to organizations what blinders are to horses.

> Sometimes lack of strategy is temporary and even necessary. It may, for example, simply represent a stage in the transition from an outdated strategy to a new, more viable one. Or it may reflect the fact that an environment has turned so dynamic that it would be folly to settle on any consistency for a time.

> Like every theory, strategy is a simplification that necessarily distorts the reality. Strategies and theories are not reality themselves, only representations (that is, abstractions) of reality in the minds of people. Thus every strategy must misrepresent and mistreat at least some stimuli.

> Eventually all situations change, environments destabilize, niches disappear. Then all that is constructive and efficient about an established strategy becomes a liability. That is why even though the concept of strategy is rooted in stability, so much of the study of strategy focuses on change.

Source: © 1987, by The Regents of the University of California. Adapted from the *California Management Review*, "The Strategy Concept II: Another Look at Why Organizations Need Strategies" by Henry Mintzberg, Vol 30, No 1. By permission of the Regents.

ARE STRATEGIES REAL THINGS?
BY BRUCE AHLSTRAND AND HENRY MINTZBERG

Maybe not, claim two of this book's authors, putting this book and all of us—writers and readers alike—into question. Strategy is treated as some kind of real thing—a conceptual artifact, if you like. Thus we hold retreats to "decide" on them, hire consultants to propose them, have CEOs present them to their boards, and hold case study discussions for students to learn about them. That way we get these things called strategies, these conceptual artifacts.

We wonder. Sure we hear about strategies, all nicely conceived and articulated. And so too do we hear about the failures of so many of them. Walter Kiechel, when he was at *Fortune*, wrote about a study that found only 10 percent of strategies successfully implemented. Tom Peters referred to this figure as "wildly exaggerated!"

Of course, failure is almost always attributed to implementation. Our strategies were clever, say the formulators; the problem is with you dumbbells in implementation. But the dumbbells might reply that if you formulators are so clever, how come you didn't formulate strategies that we dumbbells were capable of implementing. The problem, however, may lie deeper, in the very separation of formulation and implementation. Organizations don't stand still; they are dynamic entities constantly evolving. Unlike buildings, strategies do not get finished. They are works-in-progress, always changing. So their structures have to be fluid, their walls permeable. Executives cannot just hand them over to others for implementation the way

Organizations don't stand still; they are dynamic entities constantly evolving. Unlike buildings, strategies do not get finished.

architects hand over plans to builders for construction. Strategies, in other words, have to live, and so the people concerned with them had better be able to deal with them intimately, continuously. That is why the strategy process cannot be replicated in a classroom or a consulting study. Strategies from the consulting office or the case classroom, even the executive suite, often prove sterile because real strategies are about living customers and dynamic markets and evolving technologies, not about abstract strengths, weaknesses, threats, and opportunities.

Strategies from the consulting office or the case classroom, even the executive suite, often prove sterile because real strategies are about living customers and dynamic markets and evolving technologies, not about abstract strengths, weaknesses, threats, and opportunities.

Don Schön has described designing as an intimate conversation with the situation, by committed and knowledgeable people in constant search for improvement. This is quite different from "experts" looking for the right answer, the generic strategy.

The artifactual view reifies strategy, turning it into something artificially tangible. It also puts strategy on a pedestal, out of reach. Who can ask hard questions of the lofty goals and bold intentions inscribed on a pedestal? They may look good to a business press hungry for fancy strategies, even to a board marginally informed and uncomfortable about carrying out its responsibilities. But do they allow others to act better?

So should we drop the word strategy altogether, in order to focus on what really matters—products and services, customers and markets, and how they combine? Should we at least stop obsessing about strategy?

CHAPTER 2
SWOTED BY STRATEGY

"We will either find a way or make one."
(Hannibal)

"Make things as simple as possible, but not any simpler."
(Albert Einstein)

"The damn guy just sits there waiting for a case study."
(Manager about a Harvard MBA graduate)

INTRODUCTION TO CHAPTER 2

Were strategy classical music, this first view would enshrine the CEO as composer. Indeed, add a dash of drama and this becomes grand opera: full of marches and processions, building up the crescendo that reveals all.

Here strategy is created by conscious design. It is deliberate, purposeful, controlling. Key to this is SWOT—so simple, so powerful: Build on your organization's Strengths, correct its Weaknesses, seize those Opportunities, and duck the Threats in the environment. Professors worldwide, not to mention consultants and planners, have had a field day with this little model, filling untold numbers of blackboards and PowerPoint slides with their SWOT analyses, while their students "solved" hundreds of case studies. This view grew initially in the Harvard Business School, in the 1960s. In a sense, Harvard pursued its own strategy, building on its strengths in the case study method to pursue the opportunities of SWOT. Did this serve strategy? For sure. With problems.

We begin where so much has begun: with the Tower of Babel. Not the strategy Tower of Babel, the original one. The field of strategy is just repeating a long history. Then it's on to the "little black dress," a charming piece that shows vividly the power of good simple design in strategy and fashion. Next, strategy's most famous "guru" tells us why the chief executive is so important as a strategist. But is he the conductor of the strategy orchestra?

The following two bites, both fables, raise questions—one about consultants more enamored of threats and opportunities than strengths and weaknesses, the other about a mythical case study student who took Harvard at its word and bit back.

THE OTHER TOWER OF BABEL
BY JOSEPH LAMPEL

Just as we were finalizing this book, co-author Joe appeared with this little gem. How better to explain SWOT? Strategy as our own Tower of Babel.

Now the whole earth had one language and few words. And as men migrated from the east, they found a plain in the land of Shinar and settled there. And they said to one another, "Come, let us make bricks, and burn them thoroughly." And they had brick for stone and bitumen for mortar. Then they said, "Come, let us build ourselves a city, and a tower with its top in the heavens, and let us make a name for ourselves, lest we be scattered abroad upon the face of the whole earth."

On the matter of Strengths
> We speak the same language.
> We are the entertainment capital of Mesopotamia.
> We have 40 billion in Pharaonic bonds.
> We have the Great Oracle on a five-year exclusive contract.

On the matter of Weaknesses
> Our management systems are oriented toward command-and-control with little scope for initiative.
> We have virtually no competence in tower-building design.
> Our bricks are of good quality, but our mortar is the worst in the Fertile Crescent.

On the matter of Opportunities

> We can enter the tower-building business.
> This will give us sustainable competitive advantage over all of Mesopotamia.
> We will have a prestige address for camel caravans.
> The top of the tower is good for weather forecasting and astronomical observation.
> We can put a revolving garden at the top and make a sizeable income from weddings and bar mitzvahs.

On the matter of Threats

> This will tie up brick production needed for residential construction.
> The maintenance costs will be ruinous.
> This will provoke a tower-building race with Nivena.
> God may not be amused.

And the Lord came down to see the city and the tower, which the sons of men had built. And the Lord said, "Behold, they are one people, and they have all one language; and this is only the beginning of what they will do; and nothing that they propose to do will now be impossible for them. Come, let us go down, and there confuse their language, that they may not understand one another's speech." So the Lord scattered them abroad from there over the face of all the earth, and they left off building the city. Therefore its name was called Babel, because there the Lord confused the language of all the earth—some of them going forth to practice and write about strategy.

STRATEGY AS A "LITTLE BLACK DRESS"
BY JEANNE LIEDTKA

Imagine being SWOTed by a little black dress: its enticing strengths and revealing weaknesses; the opportunities that can be fantasized and their corresponding threats. Jeanne Liedtka of the University of Virginia Darden School, a big fan of design in strategy, wrote for this book the adorable little piece that follows, about the enduring allure of Coco Chanel's design. Keep it basic, keep it pure, keep it simple!

Coco Chanel is credited with the "invention" of one of the great designs of the twentieth century—the "little black dress" (or LBD), whose lessons for strategy makers are profound. Taking its inspiration from the uniforms of domestic help in Paris in the 1920s, it quickly established itself as a design of astonishing endurance in the notoriously fickle world of women's fashion. Anyone seeking to understand the qualities of a well-designed business strategy would do well to begin by understanding the enduring allure of Chanel's design.

The most striking aspect of the LBD is its simplicity. The LBD does not overprescribe, adorn, or come in numerous colors. Instead, it offers a black canvas which its wearer tailors to the function at hand: Add pearls and heels to dress up, a bright scarf and flats to dress down. The possibilities are endless, making the LBD the most functional item in a woman´s wardrobe. It goes almost anywhere, does almost anything, its versatility amazing.

But to see the LBD as primarily functional—a dull blank canvas awaiting paint—would reveal a profound ignorance of its higher qualities. For the LBD goes beyond mere simplicity to achieve elegance—in both the fashion and the theoretical sense of the word. As a design, it is parsimonious; it both lacks nothing essential and contains nothing extraneous. As Antoine Saint-Exupery has noted (about planes, not little princes), elegant design is achieved not when nothing else can be added, but when nothing else can be taken away.

Yet the story of the appeal of the LBD remains incomplete. Despite its functionality, its versatility, its elegance, how can we account for the dominance of a design taken from the uniforms of servants, available only in a color hitherto associated with mourning, that has remained unchallenged in the ultimate of faddish fields for an astonishing 70 plus years! The mind boggles and one wonders why a legion of dissertations has not already been devoted to explaining this enigma.

I believe that the final piece of the puzzle lies with the transformative properties of the design. As a woman slips into her LBD, she becomes more of the woman she aspires to be: thinner, sexier, more sophisticated. She is elevated—in an honest, nonspandex kind of way of which she can be proud. For the genius of Chanel's design lies not only with the selection of a simple cut and a slimming color, she also pioneered the use of a new fabric in the LBD—jersey. Chanel's black dress in jersey flowed where others clung, was soft where others were stiff, was sensuous where others were slutty. The outcome was stunning—simplicity, versatility, sophisticated sensuality all rolled into one little dress. It made a kind of magic that few Western women over the course of the century have been able to resist.

Business strategies designed with the little black dress model would be simple in an elegant way.

What would business strategies designed with the LBD model look like? Of course, they would be simple in an elegant way—neither incomprehensibly obtuse to all save their creators, nor mind-numbingly banal and self-evident as in wallet-sized statements of vision. They would eschew the faddish, and focus instead on basic elements of an enduring nature, incorporating a versatility and openness that invited their "wearers" to add the adornments that they saw fit to the occasion at hand. Perhaps most importantly, they would make us feel better about ourselves when we worked with them. And not in an insincere, preachy kind of "call to greatness" way, but in a quiet way that emphasized our positives while acknowledging our flaws, all in the service of offering us hope for a better/thinner tomorrow.

In doing so, the stories that these strategies tell would echo the familiar, while translating these themes into something fresh and exciting. Perhaps even making us all feel a trifle frisky as a result—confident, open to new adventures, ready to find something special right around the corner. If a little black dress can do all of that, why can't a business strategy?

THE CEO AS STRATEGIST
BY MICHAEL PORTER

Michael Porter of the Harvard Business School argues here that great strategies are a cause, and the chief executive has to lead that cause.

The chief strategist of an organization has to be the leader—the CEO. A lot of business thinking has stressed the notion of empowerment, of pushing down and getting a lot of people involved. That's very important, but empowerment and involvement don't apply to the ultimate act of choice. To be successful, an organization must have a very strong leader who's willing to make choices and define the trade-offs. I've found that there's a striking relationship between really good strategies and really strong leaders.

That doesn't mean that leaders have to invent strategy. At some point in every organization, there has to be a fundamental act of creativity where someone divines the new activity that no one else is doing. Some leaders are really good at that, but that ability is not universal. The more critical job for a leader is to provide the discipline and the glue that keep such a unique position sustained over time.

Another way to look at it is that the leader has to be the guardian of trade-offs. In any organization, thousands of ideas pour in every day: from employees with suggestions, from customers asking for things, from suppliers trying to sell things. There's all this input, and 99 percent of it is inconsistent with the organization's strategy.

Great leaders are able to enforce the trade-offs: "Yes, it would be great if we could offer meals on Southwest Airlines, but if we did that it wouldn't fit our low-cost strategy. Plus, it would make us look like United, and United is just as good as we are at serving meals." At the same time, great leaders understand that there's nothing rigid or passive about strategy—it's something that a company is continually getting better at—so they can create a sense of urgency and progress while adhering to a clear and very sustained direction.

A leader also has to make sure that everyone understands the strategy. Strategy used to be thought of as some mystical vision that only the people at the top understood. But that violated the most fundamental purpose of a strategy, which is to inform each of the many thousands of things that get done in an organization every day, and to make sure that those things are all aligned in the same basic direction.

If people in the organization don't understand how a company is supposed to be different—how it creates value compared to its rivals—then how can they possibly make all of the myriad choices they have to make? Every salesman has to know the strategy, otherwise he won't know who to call on. Every engineer has to understand it, or she won't know what to build.

The best CEOs I know are teachers, and at the core of what they teach is strategy. They go out to employees, to suppliers, and to customers and they repeat, "This is what we stand for, this is what we stand for." So everyone understands it. This is what leaders do. In great companies, strategy becomes a cause. That's because a strategy is about being different. So if you have a really great strategy, people are fired up; "We're not just another airline. We're bringing something new to the world."

Source: By Keith Hammonds © 2004 Gruner + Jahr USA Publishing. First published in *Fast Company Magazine*. Reprinted with permission.

THE MANAGER AS ORCHESTRA CONDUCTOR?

"One analogy [for the manager] is the conductor of a symphony orchestra, through whose efforts, vision and leadership, individual instrumental parts that are so much noise by themselves, become the living whole of music. But the conductor has the composer's score: he is only interpreter. The manager is both composer and conductor."

(Peter Drucker (1954) *The Principles of Management*, New York: HarperCollins 1986)

"Before we made the study, I always thought of a chief executive as the conductor of an orchestra, standing aloof on his platform. Now I am in some respects inclined to see him as the puppet in the puppet-show with hundreds of people pulling the strings and forcing him to act in one way or another."

(Sune Carlson (1951) *Executive Behaviour*, Stockholm: Stromberg)

"The manager is like a symphony orchestra conductor, endeavoring to maintain a melodious performance in which the contributions of the various instruments are coordinated and sequenced, patterned and paced, while the orchestra members are having various personal difficulties, stage hands are moving music stands, alternating excessive heat and cold are creating audience and instrumental problems, and the sponsor of the concert is insisting on irrational changes in the program."

(Leonard Sayles (1964) *Managerial Behaviour: Administration in Complex Organisations*, New York: McGraw-Hill)

THE TORTOISE AND THE HARE: A FABLE FOR SENIOR EXECUTIVES
BY JOHN KAY

Threats and opportunities, to be sure, but strengths and weaknesses? So asks John Kay in this variation of a famous fable. Clients beware; consultants can SWOT too.

Once upon a time, there was a tortoise which lived in some marshes on the edge of a large plain. The tortoise had a hard shell with an attractive lustre and had lived contentedly in the marshes for many years.

But the tortoise was happy no longer. The source of its distress was the athletics contests which were frequently organised by the animals of the plain. The tortoise did well in some events, like hide-and-seek and limbo dancing. But not in the races. In every event, from the 100 meters to the cross-country, the tortoise was left far behind by most of the other competitors. Especially by the hares.

What was to be done? Like everyone who is not sure what to do next, the tortoise turned to a firm of management consultants. It sought the advice of Boston, McBainey and Butterson, one of the best-regarded firms in the business. Within a few days, the tortoise was surrounded by youngsters with MBAs from the finest business schools. They measured the dimensions of the tortoise and the way it moved. They held in-depth interviews with other tortoises, and with hares. Above all they listened intently to the tortoise's own concerns.

Following this intensive appraisal, Boston, McBainey and Butterson went away to prepare their recommendations. Soon the consultants returned to present their findings. This time they brought a senior partner from the firm and a van full of audio-visual equipment.

They began the session with their diagnosis. The reason the tortoise kept losing races, they pointed out, was that tortoises could not run as fast as hares. They illustrated this with several PowerPoint slides, and, conclusively, with a video that showed hares regularly overtaking tortoises. The tortoise was extremely impressed. "I can see," it thought to itself, "why these young people earn such high salaries. They have learned to listen to the client and to focus exactly on the nature of its concerns."

But there was better to come. The consultants went on to explain why the tortoise could not run as fast as the hare. It was because the tortoise had short legs and a heavy body. When you put diagrams of a tortoise and a hare side by side on the screen, there could be no doubt about it. The hare had much longer legs and a lean figure.

By this time, the tortoise was rolling on its shell in delight. These people did not, like some consultants, just relay back to you what you had already told them. The clincher was an elegant diagram that summarised it all. One axis described the length of legs; the other, body weight. The best position to be in was long legs, low body weight; the worst was short legs, high body weight. There was a picture of a hare in one box, a tortoise in another, and an arrow to show how the tortoise needed to move, or reengineer itself as the consultants put it. "What relevance! What insight!" the tortoise chortled in delight.

Finally, the lights dimmed and the consultants moved to their recommendations. They showed the tortoise a picture of a jaguar. The elegance of the jaguar's graceful legs and slim body took the tortoise's breath away. So did their video, which portrayed jaguars bounding across the plain, leaving hares trailing in the far distance. What the tortoise needed to do, the consultants explained, was to turn itself into a jaguar. Short legs were only superficial manifestations of the tortoise's problem. The real obstacle to success for the tortoise was that it was constrained by the limits of its imagination. So many creatures in today's environment, the consultants explained, suffered from this deficiency; so many had been helped, by Boston, McBainey and Butterson, to overcome it.

The consultants left their (rather large) invoice on the way out, but the tortoise's first reaction was that this had been money well spent. Yet after a few days, some doubts began to penetrate even the thick shell of the tortoise. Finally, it plucked up courage to telephone Boston, McBainey and Butterson. "How exactly do I go about changing into a jaguar?" the tortoise asked.

Embarrassed at asking such a naïve question, the tortoise was relieved when the consultants offered an immediate answer. But then it remembered that good consultants always had an immediate answer.

"Many of our clients ask that," Boston, McBainey and Butterson explained, "so many, in fact, that we have just set up a new change management division to help them. These consultants are trained to explain to every part of the body the importance of turning into a jaguar. Indeed, the new program allows them to stay with a client for as long as necessary, until the change process is complete."

The tortoise was attracted by this proposition. But before returning the engagement letter to Boston, McBainey and Buttersons, it had a word with the wise old owl. And what the wise old owl told it was this. Tortoises and hares have evolved for very different environments. Hares do best in wide open spaces, where their speed gives them a competitive advantage. Tortoises survive for many years in hostile territory, where their shells protect them from predators and the weather. That is why even if the plains may sometimes look more attractive, they are attractive for hares, not for tortoises; and why equally it is not sensible for hares to come down into the marshes. A happy creature is one whose characteristics match the environment within which it operates, and that is what the gradual process of biological evolution helps to achieve.

Hares do best in wide open spaces, where their speed gives them a competitive advantage. Tortoises survive for many years in hostile territory, where their shells protect them from predators and the weather.

The tortoise thought this advice was shrewd, and trundled back into the marshes. It proved to be a wise decision. A few weeks later, a pride of lions found its way onto the plains and ate all the hares. The tortoise lived on in the marshes, slowly but happily, almost ever after.

Source: *Financial Times*, September 5, 1997.

JACK'S TURN
BY HENRY MINTZBERG

This bite takes a not-so-sympathetic look at the effect of creating strategists in case study classrooms. The story is apocryphal—no Harvard student would say what Jack said. But how many think it? (Sadly, perhaps too few.)

[In lecture courses, students] are waiting for you to give "the answer" ... What we say with the case method is "Look, I know you don't have enough information—but given the information you do have, what are you going to do?" (Lieber [1999] quoting Roger Martin, Dean of the University of Toronto Business School)

"OK Jack, here you are at Matsushita: What are you going to do now?" The professor and 87 of Jack's classmates anxiously await his reply to the cold call. Jack is prepared; he has thought about this for a long time, ever since he was told that the case study method is supposed to "challenge conventional thinking." He has also been told repeatedly that good managers are decisive, therefore good MBA students have to take a stand. So Jack swallows hard and answers.

"How can I answer that question?" Jack begins. "I barely heard of Matsushita before yesterday. Yet today you want me to pronounce on its strategy."

"Last night, I had two other cases to prepare. So Matsushita, with its hundreds of thousands of employees and thousands of diverse complicated products, got a couple of hours.

I read the case over once quickly and again, well let's say less quickly. I never knowingly used any of its products. (I didn't even know before yesterday that Matsushita makes Panasonic.) I never went inside any of their factories. I've never even been to Japan. I spoke to none of their customers. I certainly never met any of the people mentioned in the case. Besides, this is a pretty high-tech issue and I'm a pretty low-tech guy. My work experience, such as it was, took place in a furniture factory. All I have to go on are these 20 pages. This is a superficial exercise. I refuse to answer your question!"

What happens to Jack? At Harvard, I'll let you guess. But from there, he goes back to the furniture business, where he immerses himself in its products and processes, the people and the industry. He is an especially big fan of its history. Gradually, with his courage to be decisive and to challenge conventional thinking, Jack rises to become CEO. There, with hardly any industry analysis at all (that would have come in a later course), he and his people craft a strategy that changes the industry.

Meanwhile, Bill, sitting next to Jack, leaps in. He has never been to Japan either (although he did know that Matsushita makes Panasonic). Bill makes a clever point or two and gets that MBA. That gets him a job in a prestigious consulting firm where, as in the case study classes back at Harvard, he goes from one situation to another, each time making a clever point or two concerning issues he recently knew nothing about, always leaving before the implementation begins. As this kind of experience pours in, it is not long before Bill becomes chief executive of a major appliance company. (He never consulted for one, but it does remind him of that Matsushita case.) There he formulates a fancy high-tech strategy, which is implemented through a dramatic program of acquisitions. What happens to that? Guess again.

Readers [of Kelly and Kelly's book, **What They Really Teach You at the Harvard Business School** *(1986)] are probably asking—read the case and do that analysis in two to four hours? Harvard's answer is yes. Students need to prepare two to three cases each day ... So [they] must work toward getting their analysis done fast as well as done well.*

Source: *Managers Not MBAs* by Henry Mintzberg, San Francisco: Berrett-Koehler and Harlow: Pearson Education, 2004.

References
Kelly, F. and Kelly H.M. (1986) *What They Really Teach You at the Harvard Business School*, New York: Warner.

Lieber, R. (1999) "Learning and Change—Roger Martin," *Fast Company*, 30, December 1999: p. 262.

STRATEGY CAREFULLY

"Planning is deciding to put one foot in front of the other."
(Winston Churchill)

"Through the control process, we can stop managers from falling in love with their businesses."
(Planning manager in large British company)

"Doubt is not a pleasant state, but certainty is a ridiculous one."
(Voltaire)

INTRODUCTION TO CHAPTER 3

Here we come to the horoscope mentioned earlier;
strategy as the future laid out carefully. It's called
"strategic planning" and it became a virtual religion
in the 1970s, curiously enough among Communist
governments and Western corporations alike. Here is
strategy as control—of thoughts, of actions, of
people, above all of the future. Accordingly, the
SWOT model was transformed into an elaborate
sequence of steps, comprising all sorts of checklists
and techniques—a science of strategy making, if you
like. Strategies were supposed to appear from such a
process full blown and carefully articulated, so that
they could be implemented through detailed
objectives, budgets, and operating plans of all kinds.
It was the classic machine assumption, applied to
strategy: Produce all the parts, assemble them as
specified, and out comes the strategy. Of course,
experts are required, so the manager as architect of
strategy got replaced, often subtly, by teams of
planners, as the engineers of strategy.

   As strategic planning practice grew, so did
its detractors. By the late 1980s, it fell out of favor.
Many declared it to be dead and buried. Well, not so

fast. For one thing, government departments and so-called nongovernment organizations were just catching up, and many remain enamored with strategic planning as it was practiced in business in the 1970s. For another, there is a baby in that bathwater, and so planning came back in different ways.

Our first byte shows how. It describes how strategic planning came back to benefit some companies. The next two explain why it went away before that: first in the words of Jack Welch, who trashed it at General Electric, and then in the more orderly words of Ian Wilson, who describes the deadly sins of strategic planning.

But there are other ways to do it and think about it. One byte suggests we should plan in case; it's called scenario planning. Another argues that when an "in case" does come up, any old plan will do. Planning gets us going, Karl Weick claims.

But does it always get us going in the right direction? That is the message of a series of bites that follows: a poem, a chart, a speech by Mao Tse Tung, a look at planning's role in an infamous battle, and finally, to cap all this, the suggestion that there is a little magic in planning (but not as you might think!).

THE REVOLUTION IN STRATEGIC PLANNING
BY JOHN BYRNE

Strategic planning is making a comeback, wrote one of *Business Week*'s most prominent journalists in 1996.

He was in his mid-20s and had never made a product, run a business, or managed an employee. But he was armed with a Harvard University MBA and a power suit, and he had a magic talisman: He was a consultant at one of the hottest strategy boutiques of the 1970s. And after he completed a presentation on Boston Consulting Group Inc.'s strategic ideas at a major U.S. company, the young consultant got his due when the board of directors erupted into enthusiastic applause.

Those were heady times, recalls John Clarkeson, the young MBA who joined BCG from Harvard in 1966 and is now its chief executive. In its heyday, strategy spinning was the ultimate left-brain exercise for the corporate elite. Thousands of B-school-trained thinkers sat high in the climate-controlled arteries of bloated business empires, crunching numbers and spinning scenarios to conquer adversaries. The popularity of corporate strategy spawned a mini-industry of brainy consulting boutiques, and nearly every CEO worth his perks learned how to sort out his business by cows, dogs, stars, and question marks. Everything could be categorized, analyzed, quantified, and predicted. You could plot a strategy that would safely steer your company to uninterrupted triumph if only you thought hard enough.

Or maybe not. By the early 1980s, as U.S. companies found themselves battered by global competitors and more nimble entrepreneurs, the cerebral strategizing of the past looked like a luxury of a more leisurely era. Suddenly, Corporate America was frantically struggling to catch up. Instead of weaving elegant stratagems, companies were scrambling to improve quality, restructure, downsize, and reengineer.

But here's a funny thing. After more than a decade of shrinking to hike productivity and efficiency, companies are now eager to wring more profits out of those streamlined operations. So what's making a comeback? You guessed it: strategic planning. Suddenly, the idea of rising above the tumult of day-to-day business to ponder the future of markets and competitors is looking attractive again. Reengineering consultants with stopwatches are out. Strategy gurus with visions of new prospects are in . . . .

At one company after another—from Sears to IBM to Hewlett-Packard to Searle—strategy is again a major focus in the quest for higher revenues and profits. With help from a new generation of business strategists, companies are pursuing novel ways to hatch new products, expand existing businesses, and create the markets of tomorrow. Some companies are even recreating full-fledged strategic-planning groups. United Parcel Service expects to spin out a new strategy group from its marketing department, where strategic plans are now hatched. Explains Chairman Kent C. Nelson: "Because we're making bigger bets on investments in technology, we can't afford to spend a whole lot of money in one direction and then find out five years later it was the wrong direction." Many mainstream consulting firms, including one-time strategy leader BCG, say their strategy business is booming . . . .

But if strategic planning is back with a vengeance, it's also back with a difference. Gone are the abstraction, sterility, and top-down arrogance of the old model. The death knell for that

approach was sounded in 1983 when General Electric Chairman
John F. Welch dismantled the company's once-heralded planning
department, where as many as 200 senior-level staffers used to
crank out vinyl-bound reports. Welch found GE planners too
consumed with operating and financial details instead of
competitive positioning and the creation of future markets, and
too divorced from the day-to-day reality of line managers.

    Today's gurus of strategy urge companies to
democratize the process—once the sole province of a company's
most senior officers—by handing strategic planning over to teams
of line and staff managers from different disciplines. Frequently,
these teams include junior staffers, handpicked for their ability to
think creatively, and near-retirement old-timers willing to tell it
like it is. And to keep the planning process close to the realities of
markets, today's strategists say it should also include interaction
with key customers and suppliers. That openness alone marks a
revolution in strategic planning, which was always among the most
sacrosanct and clandestine of corporate activities. But it's necessary
if the process is to help produce what customers want . . . .

Today's gurus of strategy urge companies to democratize the process—once the sole province of a company's most senior officers.

    Finland's Nokia Group had been exploding at a rate of
70 percent a year in the booming telecommunications business
when it chose to involve 250 employees in a strategic review early
last year. "By engaging more people, the ability to implement
strategy becomes more viable," says Chris Jackson, head of
strategy development at Nokia. "We won a high degree of
commitment by the process, and we ended up with lots of options
we hadn't looked at in the past."

Among other things, the review forced managers to look at the convergence of different technologies and how they would affect the company. The most tangible benefit to date is the creation earlier this year of a new "smart-car" unit in Germany to develop products for the auto industry . . . .

The company's top executive team now meets monthly with a strategy agenda. Nokia also says that the line managers who spent a quarter of their time over six months on the exercise now have the training and perspective to make strategy a regular part of their jobs. "We've taken strategy away from the yearly cycle that it was in, and we're trying to make it a daily part of a manager's activity," says Jackson. "We haven't quite arrived at that yet, but we're clearly moving in that direction."

That's also the direction Jack Welch has been moving in ever since he nuked GE's central-planning department. Welch pushed responsibility for strategy down to each of GE's 12 unit heads, who meet every summer with Welch and his top management team for day-long planning sessions. "The focus is on strategy, both near-term and a four-year look into the future," says Steven Kerr, vice-president for corporate management development. "They lay out what they are going to do, what new products they are interested in, and what our competition is doing." The Corporate Executive Council, a group of GE's top 24 execs, also meets four times a year to dissect each business and where it is headed.

But there's no one at GE with the title of head of strategic planning. "If you had one, what would such a person do?" asks Kerr. "He would require reports." Bound in vinyl, no doubt. Definitely not the way the strategic-planning game is played anymore.

Source: "After a Decade of Gritty Down-Sizing, Big Thinkers are Back in Vogue" by John Byrne in *Business Week*, August 26, 1996.

JACK WELCH ON PLANNING

Jack Welch spoke for himself when he was the CEO of General Electric. Here is a small but vivid piece about a CEO hacking through formal reports and numbers to discover what's really going on.

A couple of months into the job, Art Bueche, the head of our R&D operations, stopped by my office. He wanted to give me a series of cards with written questions for our upcoming planning sessions with GE business leaders. The centerpiece of these meetings, held every July, were thick planning books that contained detailed forecasts of sales, profits, capital expenditures, and myriad other numbers for the next five years. These books were the lifeblood of the bureaucracy. Some GE staffers in Fairfield actually graded them, even assigning points to the pizazz of each cover. It was nuts.

I looked through the cards Art handed me, surprised to see corporate crib sheets filled with "I gotcha" questions.

"What the hell am I supposed to do with these?"

"I always give the corporate executive office these questions. That lets them show the operating people that they studied the planning books," he replied.

"Art, this is crazy," I said. "These meetings have got to be spontaneous. I want to see their staff for the first time and react to it. The planning books get the conversation going."

The last thing I wanted was a series of tough technical questions to score a few points. What was the purpose of being CEO if I couldn't ask my own questions? The corporate staff had its rear end to the field—and it was too busy "kissing up" to the bosses.

The corporate executive office, including my vice chairmen, wasn't the only group at headquarters getting crib sheets. For every business review, headquarters people loaded up their own staff heads with questions.

We had dozens of people routinely going through what I considered "dead books." All my career, I never wanted to see a planning book before the person presented it. To me, the value of these [planning] sessions wasn't in the books. It was in the heads and hearts of the people who were coming into Fairfield. I wanted to drill down, to get beyond the binders and into the thinking that went into them. I needed to see the business leaders' body language and the passion they poured into their arguments.

The value of these [planning] sessions wasn't in the books. It was in the heads and hearts of the people.

There were too many passive reviews. One annual ritual was the spring trip to the appliance product review in Louisville. A team of designers and engineers hauled out cardboard and plastic mock-ups. Here we were from Fairfield, being asked for our opinions on futuristic refrigerators, stoves, and dishwasher models.

I'll never know how many of these models ever made it to the dealer's selling floor. I did know that some of the mock-ups had to have the dust brushed off them because they had been paraded out in prior reviews for years. I also knew that the comments from the Fairfield contingent, including myself, were of little value. This ritual was a waste of everyone's time.

I wanted to break the cycle of these dog-and-pony shows. Hierarchy's role to passively "review and approve" had to go.

Source: *Jack: Straight From the Gut* by Jack Welch with John A. Byrne, New York: Warner Books, 2001: pp. 93–94.

THE SEVEN DEADLY SINS OF PLANNING
BY IAN WILSON

Jack Welch told it personally, Ian Wilson [at GE] tells it more systematically (can we say more planned?). He compiled a list of the seven deadly sins of strategic planning at GE.

1.   *The staff took over the process.* This situation arose partly because CEOs created new staff components to deal with a new function, partly because the staff moved in to fill a vacuum created by middle management's indifference to a new responsibility, and partly because of arrogance and empire building. As a result, planning staff all too often cut executives out of the strategy development process, turning them into little more than rubber stamps . . . .

2.   *The process dominated the staff.* The process's methodologies became increasingly elaborate. Staff placed too much emphasis on analysis, too little on true strategic insights . . . Strategic thinking became equated with strategic planning . . . Jack Welch, the chairman and CEO of GE, described the outcome graphically: "The books got thicker, the printing got more sophisticated, the covers got harder, and the drawings got better" . . . .

3.   *Planning systems were virtually designed to produce no results.* . . . . The main design failure lay in denying, or diminishing, the planning role of the very executives whose mandate was to execute the strategy . . . The attitude of many was typified by the angry retort of one executive: "The matrix picked the strategy—let the matrix implement it!" The other design fault was the failure to integrate the strategic planning system with the operations system, resulting in a strategy that did not drive action.

The matrix picked the strategy—let the matrix implement it!

4.   *Planning focused on the more exciting game of mergers, acquisitions, and divestitures at the expense of core business development.* This problem stemmed in part from the temper of the times. But it also resulted from the inappropriate use of planning tools . . . .

5.   *Planning processes failed to develop true strategic choices . . .* Planners and executives rushed to adopt the first strategy that "satisficed" (i.e., met certain basic conditions in an acceptable manner). They made no real effort to search for, or analyze, an array of strategy alternatives before making a decision. As a result, companies all too often adopted strategies by default rather than by choice.

6.   *Planning neglected the organizational and cultural requirements of strategy . . .* The process focused, rightly, on the external environment, but it did so at the expense of the internal environment that is critical in the implementation stage.

7.   *Single-point forecasting was an inappropriate basis for planning in an era of restructuring and uncertainty . . .* Companies still tended to rely on single-point forecasting. Scenario-based planning was the exception rather than the rule . . . Plans that relied on [single-point forecasting] suffered increased vulnerability to surprises . . . [Moreover] because planning assumptions spelled out a single future, one that was almost always some slight variation of an extrapolation of past trends, there was an inherent bias in favor of continuing a "momentum strategy" . . . .

Source: Reprinted from *Long Range Planning*, 27, Ian Wilson, "Strategic Planning Isn't Dead—It Changed," pp. 12–24, © 1994 with permission from Elsevier.

PLANNING IN CASE
BY LAWRENCE WILKINSON

Planning bit back. It created new, more sophisticated techniques. One is scenario planning. If you can't predict the future, then maybe you can imagine various futures. Lawrence Wilkinson provides a guide to this popular planning technique.

It happens to us all. We look out into the future, trying our best to make wise decisions, only to find ourselves staring into the teeth of ferocious and widespread uncertainties. If only everything didn't depend on, well, everything else. How do we decide what kind of career path to pursue when it's not clear what industries will exist in 10 or 15 years? How do we plan our children's education when we can't know what sort of society they'll live in? As we face each of these problems, we confront a deeper dilemma: How do we strike a balance between prediction—believing that we can see past these uncertainties when in fact we can't—and paralysis—letting the uncertainties freeze us into inactivity?

      The senior managers of large corporations face a similar dilemma, but they often carry the additional weight that on their decisions rest the livelihoods of thousands. The cliché is that it's lonely at the top. But for most managers these days, the bigger problem is that it's confusing up there. It's no longer enough simply to execute, to "do things right." Like us, senior executives have to choose *the right thing to do*: set a course, steer through the strategic issues that cloud their companies' horizons. Do we or don't we buy that competitor? Build that semiconductor fab plant? Replace the copper in our network with fiber? Or wait and save billions?

Questions like these are known as "long fuse, big bang" problems. Whatever you decide to do will play out with a big bang—often a life or death difference to an organization—but it can take years to learn whether your decision was wise or not. Worse yet, "long fuse, big bang" questions don't lend themselves to traditional analysis; it's simply impossible to research away the uncertainties on which the success of a key decision will hang.

Still, like us, the manager must make a decision and make it *now*. The rest of the stampeding world will not wait until certainty appears. Anything that can help make a decision in the midst of uncertainty will be valuable. One such tool is scenario planning. A growing number of corporate executives are using scenario planning to make big, hard decisions more effectively. And it's not just for bigwigs: scenario planning can help us at a personal level as well.

Scenario planning derives from the observation that, given the impossibility of knowing precisely how the future will play out, a good decision or strategy to adopt is one that plays out well across several possible futures. To find that "robust" strategy, scenarios are created in plural, such that each scenario diverges markedly from the others. These sets of scenarios are, essentially, specially constructed stories about the future, each one modeling a distinct, plausible world in which we might someday have to live and work.

Yet, the purpose of scenario planning is not to pinpoint future events but to highlight large-scale forces that push the future in different directions. It's about making these forces

Scenario planning derives from the observation that, given the impossibility of knowing precisely how the future will play out, a good decision or strategy to adopt is one that plays out well across several possible futures.

visible—so that if they do happen, the planner will at least recognize them. It's about helping make better decisions today.

This all sounds rather esoteric, but as my partner Peter Schwartz is fond of saying, "scenario making isn't rocket science." He should know. Not only did he help develop the technique back in the 1970s, but he's also a rocket scientist.

Scenario planning begins by identifying the focal issue or decision. There are an infinite number of stories that we could tell about the future; our purpose is to tell those that matter, that lead to better decisions. So we begin the process by agreeing on the issue that we want to address. Sometimes the question is rather broad (what's the future of the former Soviet Union?); sometimes, it's pretty specific (should we introduce a new operating system?). Either way, the point is to agree on the issue(s) that will be used as a test of relevance as we go through the rest of the scenario-making process . . . .

Since scenarios are a way of understanding the dynamics shaping the future, we next attempt to identify the primary "driving forces" at work in the present. These fall roughly into four categories:
1.   Social dynamics
2.   Economic issues
3.   Political issues
4.   Technological issues

Of course, categories are only handles. Real issues entail a bit of all four forces. The point of listing the driving forces is to look past the everyday crises that typically occupy our minds and to examine the long-term forces that ordinarily work well outside our concerns. It is these powerful forces that will usually catch us unaware. Once these forces are enumerated, we can see that from our own viewpoint, some forces can be called "predetermined"—not in a philosophical sense, but in that they are completely outside our control and will play out in any story we tell about the future. For instance, the number of high school students in California 10 years from now is more or less predetermined by the number of elementary school children now. Not all forces are so evident, or so easy to calculate, but when we build our stories, predetermined elements figure in each one.

After we identify the predetermined elements from the list of driving forces, we should be left with a number of uncertainties. We then sort these to make sure they are *critical* uncertainties. A critical uncertainty is an uncertainty that is key to our focal issue. For instance, will the percentage of women in the work force continue to increase? Our goals are twofold—we want better to understand all of the uncertain forces and their relationships with each other. But at the same time, we want the few that we believe are both most important to the focal issue and most impossible to predict to float up to the surface . . . .

Given that we don't know which scenario will unfold, what do we do to prepare?

Some of the decisions we make today will make sense across all of the futures. Others will make sense only in one or two. Once we've identified those implications that work in all of the scenarios, we get on with them in the confidence that we're making better, more robust plans. The decisions that make sense in only one or some of the scenarios are tricky. For these we want to know the "early warning signs" that tell us those scenarios are beginning to unfold. Sometimes, the leading indicators for a given scenario are obvious, but often they are subtle. It may be some legislation, or technical breakthrough, or gradual social trend. Then, of course, it is important to monitor these critical signs closely.

Ultimately, that's the power of scenario planning . . . It helps us understand the uncertainties that lie before us, and what they might mean. It helps us "rehearse" our responses to those possible futures. And it helps us spot them as they begin to unfold.

Source: "How to Build Scenarios: Planning for 'long fuse, big bang' problems in an era of uncertainty" by Lawrence Wilkinson, published in *Scenarios: The Future of the Future* special issue of *WIRED*, 1995.

FORECASTING: WHOOPS!

> "Atomic energy might be as good as our present-day explosives, but it is unlikely to produce anything more dangerous." (Winston Churchill, 1939)

> "I think there is a world market for about five computers." (Thomas J. Watson, President of IBM, 1948)

> "Not within a thousand years will man ever fly." (Wilbur Wright, 1901)

> "The cinema is little more than a fad. It's canned drama. What audiences really want to see is flesh and blood on the stage." (Charlie Chaplin, 1916)

> "[Television] won't be able to hold on to any market it captures after the first six months. People will soon get tired of staring at a plywood box every night." (W. Darryl Zanuck, 20th Century Fox studio chief, 1946)

> Researcher in the British Foreign Office from 1903 to 1950: "Year after year the worriers and fretters would come to me with awful predictions of the outbreak of war. I denied it each time. I was only wrong twice."

> Few phenomena are more remarkable, yet few have been less remarked, than the degree in which material civilization—the progress of mankind in all those contrivances which oil the wheels and promote the comfort of daily life—has been concentrated in the last half century. It is not too much to say that in these respects more has been done, richer and more prolific discoveries have been made, grander achievements have been realized, in the course of the 50 years of our own lifetime than in all the previous lifetime of the race. It is in the three momentous matters of light, locomotion and communication that the progress effected in all generations put together since the earliest dawn of authentic history." (*Scientific American*, 1868)

PLANS IN CASE YOU ARE STUCK
BY KARL WEICK

Karl Weick makes a provocative point, in a way supportive of, yet quite different from, scenario planning: that when you are lost, any old plan will do!

I can best show what I think strategy is by describing an incident that happened during military maneuvers in Switzerland. The young lieutenant of a small Hungarian detachment in the Alps sent a reconnaissance unit into the icy wilderness, it began to snow immediately, snowed for two days, and the unit did not return. The lieutenant suffered, fearing that he had dispatched his own people to death. But the third day the unit came back. Where had they been? How did they make their way? Yes, they said, we considered ourselves lost and waited for the end. And then one of us found a map in his pocket. That calmed us down. We pitched camp, lasted out the snowstorm, and then with the map we discovered our bearings. And here we are. The lieutenant borrowed this remarkable map and had a good look at it. He discovered to his astonishment that it was not a map of the Alps but a map of the Pyrenees.

This incident raises the intriguing possibility that when you are lost any old map will do. Extended to the issue of strategy, maybe when you are confused, any old strategic plan will do.

Strategic plans are a lot like maps. They animate people and they orient people. Once people begin to act, they generate

When you are lost any old map will do.

tangible outcomes in some context, and this helps them discover what is occurring, what needs to be explained, and what should be done next. Managers keep forgetting that it is what they do, not what they plan that explains their success. They keep giving credit to the wrong thing—namely, the plan—and having made this error, they then spend more time planning and less time acting. They are astonished when more planning improves nothing . . . .

When I described the incident of using a map of the Pyrenees to find a way out of the Alps to Bob Engel the executive vice-president and treasurer of Morgan Guaranty, he said: "Now, that story would have been really neat if the leader out with the lost troops had known it was the wrong map and still been able to lead them back."

What is interesting about Engel's twist to the story is that he has described the basic situation that most leaders face. Followers are often lost and even the leader is not sure where to go. All the leader knows is that the plan or the map he has in front of him is not sufficient by itself to get them out. What he has to do, when faced with this situation, is instill some confidence in people, get them moving in some general direction, and be sure they look closely at what actually happens, so that they learn where they were and get some better idea of where they are and where they want to be.

If you get people moving, thinking clearly, and watching closely, events often become more meaningful. For one thing, a map of the Pyrenees can still be a plausible map of the Alps because in a very general sense, if you have seen one mountain range, you have seen them all . . . The Pyrenees share some features with the Alps, and if people pay attention to these common features, they may find their way out. For example, most mountain ranges are wet on one side and dry on the other. Water flows down rather than up. There is a prevailing wind. There are peaks and valleys. There is a highest point, and then the peaks get lower and lower until there are foothills.

Just as it is true that if you have seen one mountain range you have seen them all, it also is true that if you have seen one organization you have seen them all. Any old plan will work in an organization because people usually learn by trial and error, some people listen and some people talk, people want to get somewhere and have some general sense of where they now are, 20 percent of the people will do 80 percent of the work (and vice versa), and if you do something for somebody, they are more likely to do something for you. Given these general features of most organizations any old plan is often sufficient to get this whole mechanism moving, which then makes it possible to learn what is going on and what needs to be done next.

The generic process involved is that meaning is produced because the leader treats a vague map or plan as if it had some meaning, even though he knows full well that the real meaning will come only when people respond to the map and do something. The secret of leading with a bad map is to create a self-fulfilling prophecy. Having predicted that the group will find its way out, the leader creates the combination of optimism and action that allows people to turn their confusion into meaning and find their way home.

The leader creates the combination of optimism and action that allows people to turn their confusion into meaning.

There are plenty of examples in industry where vague plans and projects provide an excuse for people to act, learn, and create meaning.

The founders of Banana Republic, the successful mail-order clothier, started their business by acting in an improbable manner. They bought uniforms from overthrown armies in South America and advertised these items in a catalog, using drawings rather than photographs. All of these actions were labeled poor strategy by other mail-order firms. When these three actions were set in motion, however, they generated responses that no one expected (because no one had tested them) and created a belated strategy as well as a distinct niche for Banana Republic.

Tuesday Morning, an off-price retailing chain that sells household and gift items, opens its stores when they have enough merchandise to sell and then closes them until they get the next batch. As managers followed this pattern, they discovered that customers love grand openings and that anticipation would build between closings over when the store would open again and what it would contain. These anticipations were sufficiently energizing that stores that opened intermittently for four to eight weeks sold more than equivalent stores that were open year round . . . .

Source: Karl Weick, *Sensemaking in Organizations*, 345–346, © 1995 by Sage Publications. Reprinted by permission of Sage Publications, Inc.

THE CREATION

In the beginning was the plan
And then came the assumptions
And the assumptions were without form
And the plan was completely without substance
And the darkness was upon the faces of the workers.
And they spake unto their group heads,
Saying:
"It is a crock of shit, and it stinketh."
And the group heads went unto their
section heads and sayeth:
"It is a pail of dung, and none may
abide the odour thereof."
And the section heads went unto their
managers and sayeth unto them:
"It is a container of excrement, and it is
very strong,
such that none may abide by it."
And the managers went unto their
Director and sayeth unto him:
"It is a vessel of fertilizer, and none
may abide its strength."
And the Directors went unto their
Vice-President and sayeth:
"It contains that which aids plant
growth and is very strong."
And the Vice-President, went unto
the President, and
sayeth unto him:
"It promoteth growth and it is very
powerful."
And the President went unto the Chairman
And sayeth unto him:
"This powerful new plan will actively
promote the growth and
efficiency of the company and this
area in particular."
And the Chairman looked upon
the plan,
and saw that it was good
and the plan became policy.

—Anonymous

HOW TO PLAN A STRATEGY
HENRY MINTZBERG

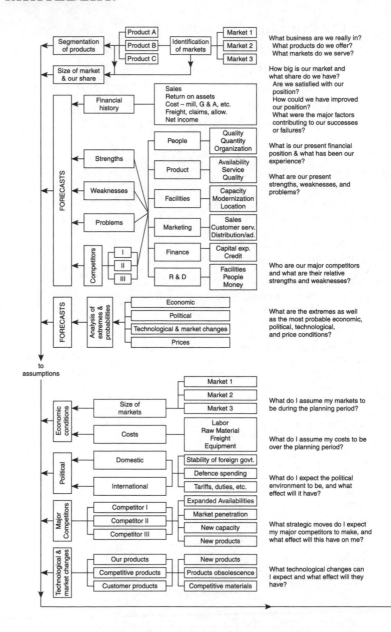

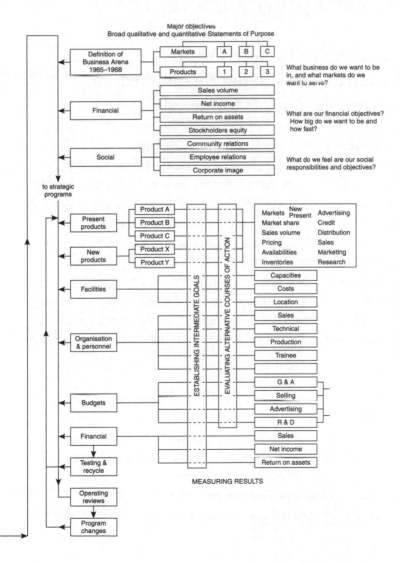

SPEECH AT THE SECOND PLENARY SESSION OF THE EIGHTH CENTRAL COMMITTEE OF THE COMMUNIST PARTY OF CHINA
MAO TSE TUNG (NOVEMBER 15, 1956)

Read this carefully; if you can figure it out, let us know. We can't. Even if it did tie hundreds of millions of people in knots for decades.

Is the first five-year plan correct? I support the opinion that it is essentially correct, as is clearly shown by the first four years of its implementation. True, there have been mistakes, but this is hardly avoidable because we lack experience. Shall we still make mistakes in the future when we have gained experience after several five-year plans? Yes, we shall. One can never acquire enough experience. Will it be possible to make no mistakes at all in planning ten thousand years hence? Things happening ten thousand years hence will no longer be our business, but one thing is certain, mistakes will be made even then ... As some comrades put it, attention has been paid only to the "bones" but very little to the "flesh."

Factory buildings have been put up and machinery and other equipment installed without the municipal construction and service facilities to go with them, and this will become a big problem in the future. In my view, its effects will be felt not during the first five-year plan, but during the second, or perhaps the third. As to whether the first five-year plan is correct, we can draw a partial conclusion now and another one next year, but I think a comprehensive conclusion will have to wait till the last phase of the second five-year plan. It is impossible to avoid some degree of subjectivism in planning. To make a few mistakes is not so bad ... On the whole, nothing seriously or fundamentally wrong has been found in the first five-year plan so far.

There should be three rounds of discussion before the annual state budget is decided. That is to say, comrades on our Central Committee and other comrades concerned should hold three meetings to discuss it and make the decision. This will enable all of us to get to understand the contents of the budget. Otherwise it will always be the comrades in charge who know them better while we on our part will just raise our hands. Yet don't we know anything about the contents? Well, I would say yes and no, we don't know very much about them. With this method of decision after three rounds of discussion, can you say you will know them very well? Not likely, and there will still be a gap between us and the comrades in charge. They are like opera singers on the stage, they know how to sing; we are like the audience, we don't know how to sing. But if we go to the opera often enough, we shall be able to tell good singers from poor ones more or less correctly. After all, it is up to the audience to pass judgment on the singer's performance. And it is with its help that the singer corrects his mistakes. This is where the audience is superior. An opera can continue to run if people like to see it over and over again. Operas which people don't like very much have to be changed. Therefore, inside our Central Committee there is the contradiction between experts and nonexperts. Experts have their strong points, and so do nonexperts. Nonexperts can tell what is right from what is wrong.

PLANNING AND FLEXIBILITY
BY HENRY MINTZBERG

Can planning be flexible? Planners claim it can; some even talk about "flexible planning." But maybe the very purpose of a plan is to be inflexible. In the following excerpts from Henry's book *The Rise and Fall of Strategic Planning*, we get glimpses of this— for better and for worse. For worse was an infamous battle of World War I, which leads into a discussion about whether processes like strategy creation can be formalized at all.

Keeping the ship on course
Consider Henri Fayol's (1949) turn-of-the-century use of the analogy of a ship at sail to emphasize planning's role in maintaining stability:

> *Unwarranted changes of course are dangers constantly threatening businesses without a plan. The slightest contrary wind can turn from its course a boat which is unfitted to resist . . . regrettable changes of course may be decided upon under the influence of profound but transitory disturbance . . . [compared with] a program carefully pondered at an undisturbed time . . . the plan protects the business not only against undesirable changes of course which may be produced by grave events, but also against those arising simply from changes on the part of higher authority. Also, it protects against deviations imperceptible at first, which end by deflecting it from its objective.*

The assumptions underlying these comments are intriguing: that change of course is a bad thing, "contrary winds" being threats and organizational responses to them being "undesirable" and "regrettable." Courses should be set in "undisturbed" times, namely before the winds begin to blow. Above all, the organization must never be deflected from its set course. A good way to deal with the occasional gust perhaps, but a heck of a way to cope with hurricanes (let alone icebergs, or news of the discovery of gold on a different island).

Of course, Fayol had gusts in mind—minor perturbations rather than major discontinuities. And he assumed the organization knew a great deal about the water in question. These are, of course, the conditions where planning makes the most sense, where the price of inflexibility is relatively low (assuming the ability to forecast accurately). As Makridakis (1990) pointed out,

> Strategy . . . should not change at the first sign of difficulty. A fair amount of persistence will be required to get beyond difficulties and problems. On the other hand, if substantial environmental changes are occurring, if competitors' reactions have been misjudged, or if the future is turning out contrary to expectations, strategy must be modified to take such changes into account. In other words, strategy must adapt: It is better to follow a side alley that leads somewhere than to finish at a dead end.

And in that case, the organization may well be advised to discard its plans as well as its formal process of planning. A common problem is that it does not.

Keeping the battle on course
The "disturbance" at the infamous World War I battle of Passchendaele was not the wind but the rain. According to Feld, it

was sunny when the plans were made at corps headquarters; as a result, 250,000 British troops fell:

> The critics argued that the planning of Passchendaele was carried out in almost total ignorance of the conditions under which the battle had to be fought. No senior officer from the Operations Branch of the General Headquarters, it was claimed, ever set foot (or eyes) on the Passchendaele battlefield during the four months that battle was in progress. Daily reports on the condition of the battlefield were first ignored, then ordered discontinued. Only after the battle did the Army chief of staff learn that he had been directing men to advance through a sea of mud. (p. 21)

To quote Stokesbury's account (1981) in his history of World War I, the "great plan" was implemented despite the effect of the steady, drenching rain on the battlefield—despite the fact that the guns clogged, that soldiers carrying heavy ammunition slipped off their paths into muddy shell holes and drowned, that the guns could not be moved forward and the wounded could not be brought backward. "Still the attack went on; they slept between sheets at corps headquarters and lamented that the infantry did not show more offensive spirit":

> [A] staff officer ... came up to see the battlefield after it was all quiet again. He gazed out over the sea of mud, then said half to himself, "My God, did we send men to advance in that?" after which he broke down weeping and his escort led him away. Staff officers ... complained that infantrymen failed to salute them. (pp. 241–242)

Who should be blamed for such a tragedy? General Haig, the British commander in charge? No doubt. But not solely. Behind him was a long tradition, especially but not only in the military, of separating strategy from tactics, formulation from implementation, thinking from acting. The ultimate enemy, once again, proves to be ourselves—not just how we behave but how we *think* about behaving.

As Feld (1959) noted in his article on the dysfunctions of traditional military organization, a sharp distinction is made between the officers in the rear, who have the power to formulate the plans and direct their execution, and the troops at the front, who, despite their first-hand experience, can implement only the plans that are given to them. One decides while the other salutes:

> *Organizations place a higher value on the exercise of reason than on the acquisition of experience, and endow officers engaged in the first activity with authority over those occupied by the second.* (p. 15)

> *The superiority of planners is based on the assumption that their position serves to keep them informed about what is happening to the army as a whole, while that of the executor limits knowledge to personal experience. This assumption is supported by the hierarchical structure of military organization which establishes in specific detail the stages and the direction of the flow of information. In terms of this hierarchy, the man who receives information is superior to the man who transmits it . . . .* (p. 22)

Unfortunately, "the conditions most favorable to rational activity, calm and detachment, stand in direct antithesis to the confusion and involvement of combat. Conditions entering into the drawing up of plans, therefore, are of a different order than those determining their execution . . . ." (p. 15) Thus, while the battle of Passchendaele may have been "strategically desirable"

The conditions most favorable to rational activity, calm and detachment, stand in direct antithesis to the confusion and involvement of combat.

it proved "tactically impossible." In other words, it worked wonderfully well—in theory. But the formulators never allowed themselves to find out, until it was too late. "The deadlock enforced by barbed wire and automatic weapons brought about an almost complete disassociation of strategic and tactical thought." But while neither "was in a position to guide the other," strategic thought had "outright dominance." (p. 21) Hence the tragedy.

The fallacy of formalization

Can the systems in fact do it? Can "strategic planning," in the words of a Stanford Research Institute economist, "re-create" the process of the "genius entrepreneur"? "I favour a set of analytical techniques for developing strategy," Michael Porter wrote in *The Economist* (May 23, 1987). But can analysis provide synthesis?

Note that strategic planning has not generally been presented as an *aid* to strategy making, or as *support* for natural managerial processes (including intuition), but *as* the former and *in place of* the latter. It is claimed to be proper practice—to borrow Frederick Taylor's (1913) favourite phrase, the "one best way" to create strategy.

There is an interesting irony in this, because planning missed one of Taylor's most important messages. Taylor was careful to note that work processes have to be fully understood before they can be formally programmed. His own accounts dwell on this at great length. But where in the planning literature is there a shred of evidence that the authors ever bothered to find out how it is that managers really do make strategy? Instead it was merely assumed that strategic planning, strategic thinking, and strategy making are all synonymous, at least in best practice. The CEO "can seriously jeopardize or even destroy the prospects of strategic thinking by not consistently following the discipline of strategic planning," wrote Lorange (1980: 12) with no support whatsoever.

The facts are first that none of those fancy planning charts ever contained a single box that explained how strategy is actually to be created—how the synthesis of those genius entrepreneurs, or even ordinary competent strategists, is to be re-created. Second, a great deal of study, much of it by researchers favorable to the process, that sought to prove that planning pays, never did prove anything of the kind. Indeed a great deal of anecdotal evidence in the popular business press suggests exactly the opposite conclusion. (And whoever met a middle manager enthusiastic about the experience: "Boy, was that strategic planning fun: I can't wait to do it next year!")

One well-known observer of the public sector, Aaron Wildavsky (1974), has concluded that PBBS, Robert McNamara's famous effort at strategic planning in the U.S. government, "failed everywhere and at all times." But that may be no less true of business, certainly if the experiences of General Electric and Texas Instruments are typical. How deeply ironic, then, that at the very same time that American business was so critical of Communism, a political structure rooted in centralized planning, it was so enamored of that very same process, and for the very same reason—the vain hope that systems could do in overgrown organizations what detached managers could not.

Third is the main argument I wish to pursue here. Formalization has not done it—"innovation" has never been "institutionalized." Quite the contrary in fact; strategic planning has more often ruined strategic thinking.

Research of my own and others tells us that strategy making is an immensely complex process involving the most sophisticated, subtle, and at times subconscious of human

"Innovation" has never been "institutionalized."

cognitive and social processes. We have found that strategy formation must draw on all kinds of informational inputs, many of them nonquantifiable and accessible only to strategists who are connected rather than detached. We know that the dynamics of the context have consistently blocked any efforts to force the process into a predetermined schedule, or onto a predetermined track. Strategies inevitably exhibit some emergent qualities, and even when largely deliberate, they often appear less formally planned than informally visionary. And learning, in the forms of fits and starts, discoveries based on serendipitous events, and the recognition of unexpected patterns, inevitably plays a key role, if not *the* key role, in the development of strategies that are novel. Accordingly, we know that the process requires insight, creativity, and synthesis; all the things that formalization discourages.

The failure of strategic planning is the failure of formalization—of systems to do better than, or even nearly as well as, flesh and blood people. It is the failure of forecasting to predict discontinuities, of programming to provide creativity, of hard data to substitute for soft, of scheduling to handle the dynamics. It has become clear that the systems have offered no improved means to deal with the information overload of human brains; indeed, often they have made matters worse. The mechanical combination of information did not solve any fundamental problem that existed with human intuition. All the promises made about "artificial intelligence," "expert systems," and the like never materialized at the strategy level. The formal systems could certainly process more information, at least hard information; they could consolidate it, aggregate it, move it about. But they could never *internalize* it, *comprehend* it, *synthesize* it. Analysis was never up to the job set for it. In a literal sense, planning never learned.

The problem in such planning systems is not any specific category so much as the process of categorization itself.

No amount of rearranging of the boxes could ever resolve the problem of the very existence of the boxes (a conclusion that can well be extended to structural reorganizations too). Strategy making, like creativity (or as creativity), needs to function beyond boxes, to create new perspectives as well as new combinations. "Life is larger than our categories," someone once quipped . . . Humpty Dumpty taught us that not everything that comes apart can be put back together again . . . .

Someone once talked about experts who avoid all the many pitfalls on the way to the grand fallacy. The grand fallacy of strategic planning is that *because analysis is not synthesis, strategic planning has never been strategy making*. Analysis may precede and support synthesis, by defining the parts that can be combined into wholes. Analysis may follow, and elaborate synthesis, by decomposing and formalizing its consequences. But analysis cannot substitute for synthesis. No amount of elaboration will ever enable formal procedures to forecast discontinuities, to inform detached managers, to create novel strategies. Thus planning, far from providing strategies, could not proceed without their prior existence. All this time, therefore, "strategic planning" has been misnamed. It should have been called "strategic programming," and promoted as a process to formalize, when necessary, the consequences of strategies already developed. Ultimately the term "strategic planning" has proved itself to be an oxymoron.

Source: *The Rise and Fall of Strategic Planning* by Henry Mintzberg, New York: Free Press, 1994. First two excerpts from pp. 186–187 and pp. 282–283. The third excerpt adapted from pp. 294 321.

References

Fayol, H. *General and Industrial Management*, London: Pitman, pp. 43–53; first published in 1916.

Feld, M. D. (1959) "Information and Authority: The Structure of Military Organization", *American Sociological Review*, XXIV, 1, 1959, pp. 15–22.

Lorange, P. (1980) *Corporate Planning: An Executive Viewpoint*, Englewood Cliffs, NJ: Prentice-Hall.

Makridakis, S. (1990) *Forecasting, Planning, and Strategy for the 21st Century*, New York: Free Press; also extracts from the 1979 draft.

Stokesbury, J.L. (1981) *A Short History of World War I*, New York: Marrow.

Taylor, F.W. (1913) *The Principles of Strategic Management*, New York: Harper and Row.

Wildavsky, A. (1974) *The Politics of the Budgetary Process*, 2nd Edition, Boston, MA: Little, Brown.

MANAGEMENT AND MAGIC
BY MARTIN L. GIMPL AND STEPHEN R. DAKIN

Maybe we plan for other reasons. Gimpl and Dakin, professors in New Zealand, contend that this is superstitious behavior, to relieve anxiety. They suggest that a good deal of forecasting is akin to magic, carrying a fruitless obsession with control into the illusion of control.

"A long range weather forecast should be obtained before leaving, as weather conditions are extremely unpredictable."

Natal Daily News, quoted in *Punch,* June 16, 1982.

There is a fundamental paradox in human behavior—the more unpredictable the world becomes, the more we seek out and rely upon forecasts and predictions to determine what we should do. It is not unreasonable to draw an analogy between weather forecasting under conditions of extreme uncertainty, and management's continuing interest in forecasting and planning activities in a highly uncertain trading climate. Why do we continue to seek forecasts when the weather is unpredictable? It is our contention that management's enchantment with the magical rites of long-range planning, forecasting, and several other

The magical rites of long-range planning, forecasting, and several other future-oriented techniques is a manifestation of anxiety-relieving superstitious behavior.

future-oriented techniques is a manifestation of anxiety-relieving superstitious behavior, and that forecasting and planning have the same function that magical rites have. Anthropologists and psychologists have long argued that magical rites and superstitious behavior serve very important functions: They make the world seem more deterministic and give us confidence in our ability to cope, they unite the managerial tribe, and they induce us to take action, at least when the omens are favorable (Perlmuter and Monty, 1977). In addition, these rites may act to preserve the status quo.

Superstitious behavior is behavior which in the eyes of a "reasonable" man is unlikely to have the causal effect it is believed to have (Jahoda, 1970). E. J. Langer (1975) refers to this as "illusion of control"—the belief that events are causally related when objectively they are not.

Superstitions increase in number and intensity as our environment becomes more uncomfortable and more unpredictable. Superstitions abound during periods of plague, famine, and warfare. B. Malinowski (1951), a social anthropologist, argued that "man resorts to magic only where chance and circumstances are not fully controlled by knowledge." To illustrate the point, he described the fishing practices of the Trobriand Archipelago. Those who are in villages in the inner lagoon, where fishing is easy and safe, do not have any magical procedures associated with it. By contrast, those in villages on the open sea, where obtaining fish is more hazardous and uncertain, have many superstitions concerning fishing.

Similarly, in today's uncertain trading climate we might expect a similar emergence of "superstitious" behavior as managers try to predict and control events which, in terms of current conditions and technology, are manifestly unpredictable and out of control. Such conditions foster the use of predictive devices ranging from capital budgeting to assessment centers. Do these devices work? If not, then we may legitimately brand their continued use as superstition.

Let us turn to some managerial behavior which we believe in time will be relegated to the ranks of superstition.

Forecasting

Foretelling the future has preoccupied man in every age. Prior to the twentieth century, the principal Western methods of forecasting included astrology, cheiromancy (palm reading), and cartomancy (reading Tarot cards) (de Givry, 1971). Minor techniques ranged from reading the entrails of slaughtered animals (practiced by the Romans among others) and reading cracks in roasted shoulder blades (Romans and Labrador Indians) to the more recently introduced methods of crystal ball gazing and reading tea leaves . . . .

If we make allowances for technical sophistication (although some ancient predictive methods are *highly* complex), it seems to us that the use of present-day forecasting procedures for predicting GDP and other time series is not far removed from the ancient techniques that are now largely discredited by our academic community.

Econometric textbooks imply that complex econometric models are more accurate for short-range forecasting than other simpler methods and, according to a survey by J. Scott Armstrong (1978), it appears that econometricians believe it. Armstrong found no empirical evidence for these beliefs and found econometric models no better than simpler naïve models . . . . .

S. Makridakis and M. Hibon (1979) measured the accuracy of various time series methods (ranging from naïve models and moving averages to Box-Jenkins techniques) on 111 different time series. The naïve models (these models simply state that next period's value adjusted for seasonability will be the same as the most recent) outperformed all of the more complex methods ... [in one popular technique] you will note the similarity to reading the heavens, tea leaves, and entrails.

In pursuing our analogy between magical rites and forecasting procedures, there is another interesting parallel. M. Gluckman (1972) notes that superstition often involves the emergence of cult-leaders, or "witch-detectives," who may direct proceedings and interpret omens. Similarly, times of uncertainty in our modern world breed magicians, witch-detectives, and consultants. Why? As John Kenneth Galbraith (1982) says:

> *In an uncertain subject matter such as economics or psychiatry, there is something wonderfully compelling about those who are sure. Also, much discussion of money has a necromantic aspect; mystery, even witchcraft, is presumed to be involved. A special reputation accrues to those who, affirming the mystery, presume to penetrate it. They are in touch with the occult; others should trust them.*

Superstitions are the vehicle whereby charismatic leaders provide feelings of certainty in otherwise uncertain times. The existence of these leaders may boost confidence, guide action, and, if things continue to go wrong, provide a scapegoat for the sufferer. The difference between modern economic forecasters and the shaman predicting and inducing rain may be more in their appearance than in the substance of their predictions ....

Implicit in the discussion so far has been the notion that superstitions are undesirable; that illusions of control should be discouraged. On the contrary, it is apparent that under certain circumstances superstitious behavior can be highly functional for both individuals and groups.

One function that may be overlooked is that, under conditions of extreme ambiguity, people may readily opt for helplessness (Perlmuter and Monty, 1977). When people feel out of control there is a tendency toward inactivity—to do nothing. Under such circumstances, of course, it is more appropriate to do something—anything—since activity may uncover elements of control which were previously unnoticed. Thus, to the extent that superstitions give the feeling of control they may encourage necessary activity.

A second major function is that in a random world the best course of action is random action. Well-designed magical rites do precisely this—they encourage random action ....

O. K. Moore (1957) tells of the use of caribou bones among the Labrador Indians. When food is short because of poor hunting, the Indians consult an oracle to determine the direction the hunt should take. The shoulder blade of the caribou is put over the hot coals of a fire; cracks in the bones induced by the heat are then interpreted as a map. The directions indicated by this oracle are basically random. Moore points out that this is a highly efficacious method because if the Indians did not use a random number generator they would fall pry to their previous biases and tend to over-hunt certain areas. Furthermore, any regular pattern of the hunt would give the animals a chance to develop avoidance techniques. By randomizing their hunting patterns the Indians' chances of reaching game are enhanced ....

There is an additional and secondary function that should be mentioned. While superstition is useful if it randomizes action, the magical rites associated with superstitions are useful in *justifying* random action. Devons has noted how difficult it is for government or nationalized industry to plan sensibly, and says:

> *No Chancellor of the Exchequer could introduce his proposals for monetary and fiscal policy in the House of Commons by saying, "I have looked at all the forecasts, and some go one way, some*

another; so I decided to toss a coin and assume inflationary tendencies if it came down heads and deflationary if it came down tails."

Thus, magical rites, including the use of economic statistics, permit managers to justify taking random action.

Having said all this, it is clear that many managerial superstitions are *dys*functional. The basic reason for their dysfunctionality is that, while they reduce anxiety and build confidence in times of uncertainty, they may simply provide justification for continuing past practice rather than sanctioning innovation. Most techniques do not generate random data but introduce a biased series—the caribou are likely to pick up your pattern.

Source: © 1984, by The Regents of the University of California. Reprinted from the *California Management Review*, "Management and Magic" by M.L. Gimpl and S.R. Dakin, Vol 27, No 3. By permission of the Regents.

References
Armstrong, J. S. (1978) "Forecasting with Econometric Methods: Folklore versus Fact," *Journal of Business*, Vol. 51, 4, 1978, pp. 549–564.

Devons, E. (1961) *Essays in Economics*, London: Allen and Unwin.

Galbraith, J. K. (1982) "You can't argue with a monetarist,' a feature article in *The Christchurch Press*, 23 September 1982; from the London Observer Service.

de Givry, G. (1971) *Witchcraft, Magic and Alchemy*, New York: Dover; first published in French, 1931.

Gluckman, M. (1972) *The Allocation of Responsibility*, Manchester University Press, p. 37.

Jahoda, G. (1970) *The Psychology of Superstition*, New York: Pelican, p. 127.

Langer, E. J. (1975) "The Illusion of Control," *Journal of Personality and Social Psychology*, 32, 1975, pp. 311–328.

Makridakis, S. and Hibon, M. (1979) "Accuracy of Forecasting; An Empirical Investigation," *Journal of the Royal Statistical Society* (A), 142, 2, 1979, pp. 97–145.

Malinowski, B. (1951) *Magic, Science, Religion and Other Essays*, quoted in Romans, G. C., *The Human Group*, London: Routledge Kegan Paul, pp. 321–323.

Moore, O. K. (1957) "Divination—A New Perspective", *American Anthropologist*, 59, 1957, pp. 69–74.

Perlmuter, L.C. and Monty, R.A. (1977) "The Importance of Perceived Control: Fact or Fantasy?" *American Scientist*, 65, 1977, pp. 959–964.

"All astrologers are liars. Even when an astrologer tells the truth, he is lying."

Proverb

CHAPTER 4
FIGURING STRATEGY

"Dream, meine Herren, but then check."
(Mario Bunge)

"It requires an unusual mind to make an analysis of the obvious."
(Alfred North Whitehead)

"It is a capital mistake to theorize before one has data."
(Sir Arthur Conan Doyle)

"In science as in love, a concentration on technique is quite likely to lead to impotence."
(Berger)

INTRODUCTION TO CHAPTER 4

Planning may have faltered, but analyzing didn't.
Indeed, it became far more popular. After the planner
had replaced the manager, or at least tried to, the
analysts replaced both—often in the guise of manager.
Management became calculating; strategizing became
figuring. And strategies themselves became
positions—places for products in markets.

    All, again, for better and for worse. There
are lots of good ideas here. But they are often
embedded in analysis for its own sake. As strategies
became positions, specifically "generic" positions, off-
the-rack, so to speak, the process of strategy making
became one of selection instead of invention.
In other words, companies copied rather than
created. All this was a boon to consultants, ready to
figure, with techniques galore, wading in hard data.

    Our first byte is intended to help you make
sense of all the concepts coming and going in this
view of strategy, using the metaphor of a rocket fired
into a market. Then we move on to a light-hearted
little case, "Toilet Nirvana" in Japan, about
positioning the derrière. Two bites that raise
questions about all this figuring follow; the first
about the soft underbelly of hard data, the second
about the potential mindlessness of easy technique.

LAUNCHING STRATEGY
BY HENRY MINTZBERG

Concepts galore—dare we say buzzwords—characterize this figuring view of strategy. They come and go out at an alarming pace. So this first byte provides a glossary by using the metaphor of a product launched into the market. This is, after all, a rather macho view of strategy.

In the large literature of strategic management that deals with positioning, the concepts come and go at a frantic pace. There is thus a need to pin them down—to develop a framework to see them all, as well as to provide a "glossary" of what they are, even for experts who tend to beaver away in one area or another. There is woefully little synthesis in the world of analysis!

Thus, a little model is offered here. It is visual because, in a sense, all of this needs to be seen to be believed. The model is a metaphor of sorts, consisting of a *launching* device, representing an organization, that sends *projectiles*, namely products and services, at a landscape of *targets*, meaning markets, faced with *rivals,* or competition, in the hope of attaining *fit*.

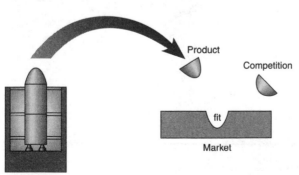

The vehicle (organization)

The organization is depicted as a launching device that develops, produces, and distributes its products and services into markets. To do that, it performs a series of *business functions* that sequence themselves into what Michael Porter (1985) has labeled a *value chain*. As depicted in our figure, design (of product and process) and production are the basic platform, while supply and sourcing (including financing) form one tower, and administration and support (such as public relations and industrial relations) form the other. The launch vehicle has two booster rockets (which fall away during the product's voyage)—the first for sales and marketing, the second for physical distribution.

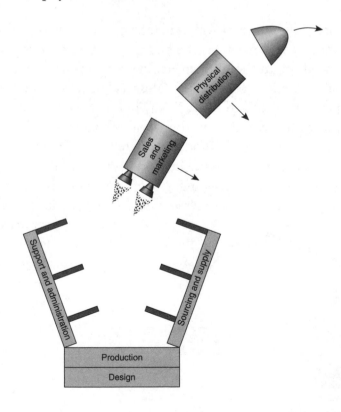

The business functions are executed by using a bundle of core *competences* or *capabilities* of various kinds (such as the ability to do research or to produce products inexpensively) and supported by all sorts of *resources* or *assets* (including patents, machinery, and so on).

Current popular theory has it that the organization should shed as many of its noncore competences as it can, in order to become lean and flexible, and so be able to focus attention on doing what it does best. The rest should be bought from suppliers. Thus, the old strategy of *vertical integration*—encompassing your suppliers *upstream* as well as your intermediate customers *downstream* so that you can control their activities tightly—gets replaced by the new one of *outsourcing*, resulting in the *virtual organization*.

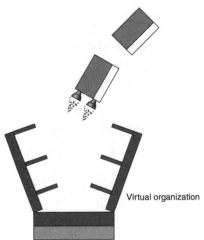

Virtual organization

Competences can be combined in various ways; for example, through *joint ventures* or other forms of *alliances* with partners, *licensing* agreements, *franchising* relationships and *long-term contracts*, the extensive combinations of which result in *networks*.

The projectile (products and services)
Proceeding along the value chain eventually creates a product (or service) which is launched at a target market. The ways in which this can be done are described by a set of *generic strategies* according to the nature of the projectile (size, shape, surrounding, etc.) and the sequence of projectiles launched (frequency, direction, etc.). First are the generic strategies that characterize the product itself:

Low cost or **price differentiation strategy**
(meaning high volume, commodity-type production)

Image differentiation strategy
(e.g., nice packaging)

Support differentiation strategy
(e.g., provision of after-sales service)

Quality differentiation strategy (e.g., more durable, more reliable, higher performance)

Design differentiation strategy
(i.e., difference in function)

Then there are the strategies that elaborate or extend the range of products offered:

Penetration strategy (targeting the same product more intensely at the same market; for example, through increased advertising)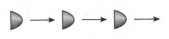

Bundling strategy (selling two products together, such as computer software with hardware)

Market development strategy (targeting the same product at new markets)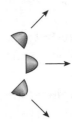

Product development strategy (targeting new products at the same market)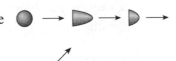

Diversification strategy (targeting different products at different markets)

The target (markets)
Here we show the generic characteristics of markets (the targeted place), first by size and divisibility, then by location, and finally by stage of evolution or change:

Mass market (large, homogeneous)

Fragmented market (many small niches)

Segmented markets (differing demand segments)

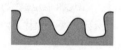

Thin market (few, occasional buyers, as in nuclear reactors)

Geographical markets (looked at from the perspective of place)

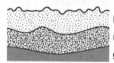
local
regional
global

Emerging market (young, not yet clearly defined)

Established (mature) market (clearly defined)

Eroding market

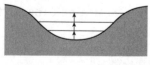

Erupting market (undergoing destabilizing changes)

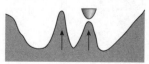

Industry and group

Where does one market end and another begin? Economists spend a lot of time worrying about identifying industries (through the definition of SIC [Standard Industrial Classification, analogous to North American Industry Classification, or NAICS] codes and the like). However, much of this is arbitrary, since they often no sooner find one than a strategist destroys it.

In our terms here, an industry can be defined as a landscape of associated markets, isolated from others by blockages in the terrain. In the literature of economics and strategic positioning, these are known as *barriers to entry*—for example, some kind of special know-how or close ties to the customers that keep potential new competitors out. Michael Porter (1980) elaborated on this with his notion of *strategic group*, really a kind of subindustry housing companies that pursue similar strategies (for example, national news magazines, as opposed to magazines targeted at specific audiences, such as amateur photographers). These are distinguished by *barriers to mobility*, in other words, difficulties of shifting into the group even though it is within the overall industry. These concepts map easily into our metaphor, with higher barriers shown for industries and lower ones for strategic groups.

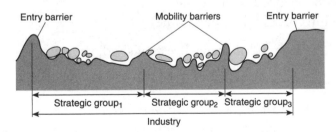

The fit (strategic positions)

When products and markets (projectiles and targets) come together, we reach the central concept of strategic management, namely *fit*, or the strategic position itself—how the product sits in the market. Fit is logically discussed, first in terms of the match between the breadth of the products offered and markets served (which Porter calls *scope*). After this, we shall turn to the quality of the fit and ways to improve it:

Commodity strategy targets a (perceived) mass market with a single, standardized product

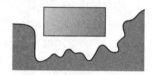

Segmentation strategy targets a (perceived) segment market with a range of products, geared to each of the different segments

Niche strategy targets a small isolated market segment with a sharply delineated product

Customization strategy (the ultimate in both niching and segmentation designs or tailors each specific product to one particular customer need, such as the architecturally designed home)

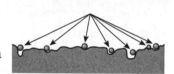

Once fit, or scope, is established, then attention turns to its strength, namely how secure it is—its durability, or *sustainability*.

First of all, we identify *natural fit*—where the product and market fit each other quite naturally, whether it was the product that created the market or the market that encouraged the development of the product. Natural fit is inherently sustainable (for example, because there is usually intrinsic customer loyalty, perhaps secured by high switching costs).

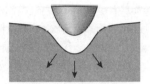
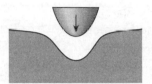

Natural fit: product push	Natural fit: market pull

This can be distinguished from *forced fit*, as well as *vulnerable fit*, which is weak and so easily dislodged, whether by attack from competitors or loss of interest from customers.

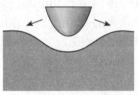

Forced fit	Vulnerable fit

When fit is not perfect (as is always true in an imperfect world) and so not easily sustainable, attention has to be given to what can be called *reinforcing mechanisms* to improve it, or *isolating mechanisms* to protect it. Inspired by the metaphor itself, we suggest three types of these:

Burrowing strategy (driving into the market deeper, for example, by using advertising to strengthen brand loyalty—but this could prove costly)

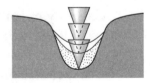

Packing strategy (tightening the fit by adding supporting elements, such as strong after-sales services, or the use of supporting brands—but the seller can get stuck, too)

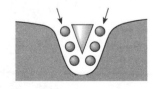

Fortifying strategy (building up barriers or *shelters* around the fit, such as seeking tariff or patent protection, or creating long-term contracts with customers—but these can topple, or else in fact blind the seller to changes occurring elsewhere)

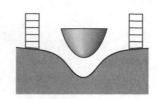

There can be a *learning strategy* to improve fit through adaptability, for example, by riding an *experience curve* to take advantage of the steady stream of learning that comes from producing more and more of the product, or getting to know customers better, or by taking advantage of the *complementarities* of a strategy that reinforce each other, such as franchising and mass preparation in fast-food retailing.

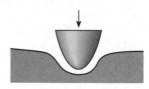

Of course, there can also be *misfit*.

Capacity misfit (what is offered exceeds what the market can take)

Competence misfit (the competences of the producer do not match the needs of the market)

Design misfit (the design is wrong for the market)

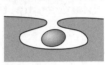

Sunk misfit (being stuck in a market due to *exit* barriers, such as dedicated machinery that cannot be used elsewhere)

Myopic misfit (the producer cannot see the market—perhaps because of too much concentration on other markets)

Location misfit (the producer is in the wrong place and cannot reach the market—perhaps because some barrier is too high)

Rivalry (competition)

So far, almost all these relationships have been between a single seller and one or more target markets. But sellers are no more found alone than are buyers. There is *rivalry* in markets, consisting of *competitors*—capable of doing better or doing differently. So we return to economics to describe various competitive situations.

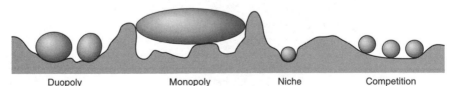

Duopoly   Monopoly   Niche   Competition

Market leader (or *dominant firm*)

Stable competition

Multipoint competition (ability to take action in one market to influence a competitor's action in another)

Unstable competition (in a mature market)

Unstable competition (in an emerging market)

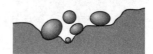

Contestability

Obviously, markets are *contestable*. New competitors can seek to drive themselves in. Here we draw especially on the literature of military strategy.

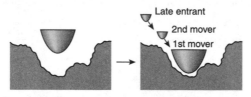

First movers seek to position themselves in new markets to keep rivals out. But *late entrants* (including *second movers*) come along and seek a share, if not displace their rivals altogether. (*Strategic window* refers to the period of opportunity when an initial or late move becomes possible, for example, during a strike in a rival's factory.) Late entrants use various military-type strategies:

Frontal attack (by the *concentration of forces*, e.g., cost cutting)

Lateral (or *indirect* or *flanking*) **attack**, perhaps by

> undermining (e.g., taking away the least-loyal customers through lower prices)

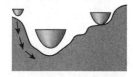

> attacking a supporting brand (to dislodge the main one)

> attacking fortifications, through a *battering strategy* (e.g., lobbying for the elimination of tariff barriers)

Guerrilla attack (series of small "hit-and-run" attacks, such as sudden moves of deep discounting)

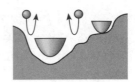

Market signalling by feint (giving the impression of doing something, such as pretending to expand plant to scare off a potential competitor)

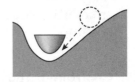

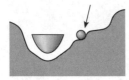

Late entrants may also seek to carve out small territories through niche strategies (sometimes called "picking up the crumbs").

Finally, rivals may reach an accord with the existing players so that all settle down to a *collaborative strategy*, perhaps in a cozy price-fixing or market-allocating *cartel*.

The truly creative strategist, however, shuns all of these categories, or at least recombines them in innovative ways to develop a *novel strategy*, for which there is no diagram since no one can tell what it might look like!

Source: "A Guide to Strategic Positioning" in H. Mintzberg, J. Lampel, J. B.Quinn, and S. Ghoshal, Eds., *The Strategy Process: Concepts, Contexts and Cases*, Upper Saddle River, NJ: Prentice Hall, 2003: pp. 127–138.

References
Porter M.E. (1980) *Competitive Strategy: Techniques for Analyzing Industries and Competitors*, New York: Free Press.

Porter M. E. (1985) *Competitive Advantage: Creating and Sustaining Superior Performance*, New York: Free Press.

POSITIONING THE DERRIÈRE: TOILET NIRVANA
BY JAMES BROOKE

How better to convey strategy as "positioning" than with an article about toilets, specifically about the toilet wars among Japanese manufacturers.

Japan's toilet wars started in February, when Matsushita engineers here unveiled a toilet seat equipped with electrodes that send a mild electric charge through the user's buttocks, yielding a digital measurement of body–fat ratio.

Unimpressed, engineers from a rival company, Inax, counterattacked in April with a toilet that glows in the dark and whirs up its lid after an infrared sensor detects a human being. When in use, the toilet plays any of six soundtracks, including chirping birds, rushing water, tinkling wind chimes, or the strumming of a traditional Japanese harp. In a Japanese house, "the only place you can be alone and sit quietly is likely to be the toilet," said Masahiro Iguchi, marketing chief for Inax . . . .

Matsushita . . . introduced in May a $3,000 throne that not only greets a user by flipping its lid, but also by blasting its twin air nozzles—air-conditioning in the summer, heat in the winter. Patting this Cadillac of toilets, Hiroyuki Matsui, chief engineer, said, "You can bring a bathroom temperature down by 7 degrees Celsius in 30 seconds."

Then in June, Toto, Japan's toilet giant, came out with *Wellyou*, a toilet that automatically measures the user's urine sugar levels by making a collection with a little spoon held by a retractable, mechanical arm.

Whether a home medical center or a Zen space for meditation, the toilet of the future will probably emerge from laboratories like the ones here at the Matsushita Electric Industrial Company—workshops so secretive and competitive that a visiting reporter and photographer were not allowed inside.

Americans should prepare for more than that simple twentieth-century choice; to flush or not to flush. Users of the Matsushita toilet can program it to preheat or precool a bathroom at a specific time at a set temperature. For owners who might not be so regular, this toilet allows users to set the temperature and pressure of a water jet spray used to wash and massage the buttocks, an enormously popular feature in Japan.

Americans should prepare for more than that simple twentieth-century choice; to flush or not to flush.

Toilet jet sprays, which sometimes confuse foreign visitors with disastrous results, are now in nearly half of Japanese homes, a rate higher than that of personal computers.

To some, this is a sign of a nation gone perilously soft. They worry that the cosseted Japanese youths of the future, sitting dreamily on air-conditioned thrones, will be no match for their squat-toilet neighbors—the worker bees of industrial China or the spartan soldiers of North Korea.

Hideki Nishioka, a 90-year-old retired professor who chairs the Japan Toilet Association, a private group, says he always recommends that new schools in Japan contain "at least one or two of the old-style squat toilets." ...

But in a country with the demographics of Florida, the real growth will be medical toilets linked to the Internet.

"You may think a toilet is just a toilet, but we would like to make a toilet a home health-measuring center," Mr. Matsui, the Matsushita engineer, said in a lecture here in Nara, near Osaka. "We are going to install in a toilet devices to measure weight, fat, blood pressure, heart beat, urine sugar, albumin, and blood in urine."

The results would be sent from the toilet to a doctor by an Internet-capable cellular phone built in to the toilet. Through long-distance monitoring, doctors could chart a person's physical well-being . . . .

But some civil libertarians are having nightmares about "smart toilets" running amok, e-mailing highly personal information hither and yon. There are also Big Brother nightmares about master computers monitoring millions of bowel movements, checking around the clock to see who is constipated, who is not eating his peas, and who is drinking too much.

"I assume the records that come out of my toilet will have the same degree of protection as records that are generated when I take a medical exam," said Lawrence Repeta, a director of the Japan Civil Liberties Union. "There will be police investigators who see this as a great tool to find people who use illegal substances."

Source: Originally published as, "Japanese Masters Get Closet to Toilet Nirvana" by James Brooke. Copyright © 2002 by the New York Times Co. Reprinted with permission.

THE SOFT UNDERBELLY OF HARD DATA
BY HENRY MINTZBERG

"If you can't measure it, you can't manage it." So the saying goes. This bite suggests that if you can only measure it, you'd better not manage it.

When data is "hard"—documented, quantified—planners and managers can sit in their offices and be informed. No need to go out and meet the troops, or the customers, to find out how the products are being bought or the war is being fought. That just wastes valuable time. This is the age of the computer; the system will do it. Or will it? I believe that hard data seriously distorts any strategy-making process that relies on it.

Study after study has demonstrated that managers of every sort rely primarily on oral forms of communication, on the order of about 80 percent of their time. Why? The answer lies in the weaknesses of hard data.

1. **Hard information is often limited in scope, lacking richness**. Formal information tends to provide the basis for description but not explanation (for example, revealing that sales were lost but not what drove the buyers away). That is why a conversation with a single disgruntled customer can sometimes be worth more than a big marketing research report. Moreover, the emphasis on quantification tends to discourage the consideration of a whole range of factors, softer but no less critical for strategy making . . . .

A conversation with a single disgruntled customer can sometimes be worth more than a big marketing research report.

The point is that much information important for strategy making never does become hard fact. The expression on a customer's face, the mood in the factory, the tone of voice of a government official, all of this can be information for the manager but not for the system. That is why managers generally spend a great deal of time developing their own *personal* information systems, comprising networks of contacts and informers of all kinds, including employees, customers, suppliers, government officials, competitors, and many others.

2.   Much hard information is too aggregated to be of effective use in strategy making. The obvious solution for a manager overloaded with information and pressed for the time necessary to process it, is to have the information aggregated. And as the organization gets larger, and the managerial level higher, more and more information must be aggregated. On to the forest instead of the trees.

The fallacy of relying on hard information lies in the assumption that nothing is lost in the process of aggregation. The reality is that a great deal is lost, often the essence of the information. It may be fine to see forests, but only so long as nothing is going on among the trees. Even lumber companies cannot make strategy by looking only at the forests. They need to study the wood and the terrain, and many other details . . . .

3.   Much hard information arrives too late to be of use in strategy making. Information takes time to "harden." Time is required for trends and events and performance to become recorded as "facts," more time for these facts to be aggregated into reports, even more time if these reports are to be presented on a predetermined schedule. Thus hard information is fundamentally historical; it reflects what happened in the past. But strategy making has to be an active, dynamic process, often unfolding quickly in reaction to immediate stimuli. As a result, oftentimes, while managers are waiting for information to harden, competitors are running off with valued customers, workers are staging wildcat strikes, and new technologies are undermining existing product lines. The world is hardly prepared to wait for information to get itself into a form acceptable to the planners and their systems . . . .

The world is hardly prepared to wait for information to get itself into a form acceptable to the planners and their systems.

A business manager has to know the real customers, not just their historical buying habits, just as a politician has to understand the mood of the people, not some sterile polling of voter preference. These are the reasons why managers bypass formal systems to create their own informal ones, and why gossip, hearsay, and speculation form such a large part of every effective manager's informational diet . . . .

4.   **Finally, a surprising amount of hard information is unreliable**. Soft information is supposed to be unreliable, subject to all kinds of biases. Hard information, in contrast, is supposed to be tangible and precise; it is, after all, transmitted and stored electronically. In fact, hard information can be no better and is oftentimes far worse than soft information.

Hard information can be no better and is oftentimes far worse than soft information.

Something is always lost in the process of quantification—before those electrons are activated—not just in the rounding-out of numbers but in the conversion of confusing events into numerical tabulations in the first place. Quantitative measures, noted Ijiri, Jaedicke, and Knight (1970), who wrote from within the accounting field, are only "surrogates" for reality. And some are rather crude. Anyone who has ever produced one—whether a reject count in a factory as a surrogate for product quality, a publication count in a university as a surrogate for research performance, or estimates of costs and benefits in a capital budgeting exercise—knows just how much distortion is possible, intentional as well as unintentional.

In his account of "statistics and planning" for aircraft production in the Air Ministry of the British government during World War II, Devons (1950) presents a litany of horror stories. The collection of such data was extremely difficult and subtle, demanding "a high degree of skill," yet "was treated ... as inferior, degrading and routine work on which the most inefficient clerical staff could best be employed" (p. 134). Errors entered the data in all kinds of ways, even just treating months as normal although almost all included some holiday or other. "Figures were often merely a useful way of summing up judgment and guesswork," and were sometimes based on "quite arbitrary assumptions," even developed through "statistical bargaining," in which officials compromised their estimates (p. 155). A guess "hazarded" in the past "quite rashly" was sometimes seized on and perpetuated (p. 156).

But "once a figure was put forward ... it soon became accepted as the 'agreed figure,' since no one was able by rational argument to demonstrate that it was wrong and suggest a better figure to replace it" (p. 155). And when these figures were portrayed in charts and used by people who did not understand them, all kinds of strange behaviors resulted, including one case where an official eyeballed a line, reflected that it was "too steep at the end," and asked that 10 percent be "knock[ed] off" the later months: that "became the official aircraft programme!" (p. 163).

The problem was the strong tendency "to assume that anything expressed in figures must necessarily be precise ... And once the figures were called 'statistics' they acquired the authority and sanctity of Holy Writ" (p. 155).

"Figures," Devons argued "gave the processes by which decisions were reached an apparent air of scientific rationality. A document which contained statistics was nearly always considered superior to one which was mere words ... For to have recognized the inadequacy of the figures would have meant admitting that policy decisions were not being taken on a rational basis." (pp. 150, 158).

Of course, soft information has problems too. Much of it is speculative; it relies on human memory, which can be fuzzy; it is subject to all kinds of psychological distortions. Ideally, strategy making draws on both kinds of information, hard and soft. But there are also times when managers have to rely on the soft kind. For example, what sales manager faced with a choice between today's rumor that a major customer was seen lunching with a competitor and tomorrow's fact that the business was lost would hesitate to act initially on the former? And, as suggested earlier, a single story from one disgruntled customer may be worth more than all those reams of market research data simply because, while the latter may identify a problem, it is the former that can suggest the solution. Overall, while hard information may inform the intellect, it is largely soft information that generates wisdom.

Source: *The Rise and Fall of Strategic Planning*, by Henry Mintzberg, New York: Free Press, 1994, pp. 257–266.

References
Devons, E. (1950) *Planning in Practice, Essays in Aircraft Planning in War-Time*, Cambridge: The University Press.

Ijiri, Y., Jaedicke, R. K. and Knight, K. E. (1970) "The Effect of Accounting Alternatives on Management Decisions" in A. Rappaport, Ed., *Information for Decision-Making*, Englewood Cliffs, NJ: Prentice Hall, pp. 421–435.

THE GLORY OF NUMBERS

> "Public agencies are very keen on amassing statistics—they collect them, add them, raise them to the nth power, take the cube root, and prepare wonderful diagrams. But what you must never forget is that every one of those figures comes in the first instance from the village watchman, who just puts down what he pleases." (Sir Josiah Stamp)

> "A mathematics professor was asked by his students to give the next member in the sequence 32, 38, 44, 48, 56, 60. He was told that the properties of the sequence were well known to him and that the solution is simple. The professor came up with a complicated polynomial after much effort, and gave up when he could not generate a simpler solution. The answer was "Meadowlark," the elevated stop after 60th Street in the city subway. The professor rode the subway daily—and got off at Meadowlark." (from C. West Churchman)

> One of the subjects of Kinsey's study of sexual behavior in the human male, afterward complaining bitterly of the injury to his masculine ego: "No matter what I told him, he just looked me straight in the eye and asked, 'How many times?'" (in Kaplan, *The Conduct of Inquiry*)

> "I stood up to be counted, and they told me to take a number."

REVERSING THE IMAGES OF BCG's GROWTH/SHARE MATRIX
BY JOHN SEEGER

Beware of technique too, not just numbers. We all know about that (for example "the rule of the tool"— that if you give a little boy a hammer, everything looks like a nail). Too many organizations these days look like smashed up beds of nails. John Seeger (of Boston College) tells us about this colorfully, using as his foil the Boston Consulting Group's "growth/share matrix," so fashionable in the 1970s. The technique may not be new, but Seeger's message is timeless.

      The growth/share matrix considered how to allocate funds to the different businesses of a company, and which strategy each should pursue. According to the matrix, it all depended on market share and growth potential. The business with a high market share and slow growth potential was to be designated a "cash cow," so that its profits could be milked and re-invested in high-growth businesses. The business with a low market share and slow growth potential was a "dog"—essentially worthless, to be liquidated. The high-share, high-growth business, in contrast, was a "star"; it was to be looked after very carefully. The low-market share, high-growth business was a "question mark" or "problem child," because it tended to require more cash than it could generate.

With this matrix, strategy became easy. Slot your business into a box, and move your money around accordingly, especially from the cash cows to the stars. But John Seeger begged to disagree. It was not so simple for all those companies that failed with the formula.

Simple concepts can easily be oversimplified, and graphic descriptors can become stereotypes. Few current business concepts are more prone to oversimplification than the growth/share model, with its labelling of products or divisions or whole companies as "dogs," "question marks," "stars," or "cash cows." Three-quarters of those labels are subject to dangerous misapplication, because popularized versions of the BCG philosophy and its derivatives carry a handy prescription for each category: We should kick the dogs, cloister the cows, and throw our money at the stars. Only the question mark category demands management thought.

This commentary attempts to counter these superficial prescriptions by turning the BCG model's own images back upon themselves. If the tendency to oversimplify comes from the language's imagery, then we must make the images do double duty; they must remind the student and manager of the growth/share matrix's pitfalls as well as its presumptions.

Every dog has its day

Consider the "dogs." In the BCG model these are the portfolio components which have low market shares and whose markets themselves are matured or shrinking; these are components we should dispose of, for they are going nowhere. The image conveyed by BCG's term is that of a feral beast preying on our resources or of a mangy cur slinking off with our picnic hotdogs.

But there are other kinds of dogs—warm, loving companions of humanity since the time of the caves. These dogs give unquestioning loyalty to their managers, serving as scouts or watch dogs, to spread the alarm if intruders threaten. By establishing a presence—with bared teeth if necessary—these friendly dogs prevent their wild cousins from approaching our picnic at all. They protect our weaker members and occupy the territory so that attackers will keep their distance. Our own dogs can repay handsomely a small investment in dog food and flea powder . . . .

"It's a dog" (says one CEO of his key retail product line). "I only wish I could get rid of it." Such attitudes are easily sensed, by canines or humans. It is predictable that the managers of his company regard its retail division as the least-attractive assignment in the company. Good managers do not willingly stay with an organization which is defined in the boss's eyes as hopeless.

Divesting this retail division would be analogous to a fire engine company's disposing of its Dalmation hound. The dog does not contribute much to the direct function of putting out fires. But it looks good in photographs; it makes life more pleasant for the firefighters during their boring waits for alarms; and it keeps other dogs from pissing on the equipment.

What do you get from a cash cow?

Consider the "cash cow." In the BCG model this is a business component which does dominate its market, but whose market is not growing. Since growth cannot logically be expected here, the consultants' advice is to operate the business as a cash-flow generator. Management should deny requests for new resources from a "cash cow" component, and concentrate on milking it for the highest possible returns.

The imagery conveyed by this term is doubly unfortunate. In oversimplified form, the "cash cow" brand can result in the gradual wastage of both the physical and human resources of an organization, as operating management learns not to request new resources and top management learns not to demand continual replenishment of the unit's productive capacities ... The creative energy required for continual renewal can decay as natural attrition suits the culture of the organization to its "cash cow" role.

In effect, classification as a cash cow may be the equivalent, over time, of placing the unit in a cloister where distractions of the outside world are minimized and all attentions are focused on the single goal, generation of high cash flows. "Milking managers" will be expert at feeding the cow and keeping it healthy in the short run. They may not be adept at maintaining the barn, however. Particularly where large outlays are needed for long-term improvements, the cash cow manager is likely to postpone investments which would hurt cash flow in the short run.

Keeping creativity, innovation and energy at high levels in an organization designated as a cash cow is an unsolved problem. One possible solution is suggested by another look at the

Keeping creativity, innovation and energy at high levels in an organization designated as a cash cow is an unsolved problem.

BCG symbolism. A cow can give more than milk; properly exposed to outside influences and environmental forces, a cow can also give calves.

The investment needed to produce a calf, given that you already have a cow, is incredibly small; without a cow, no amount of investment will do the job. Similarly, the investment needed to produce creative ideas, given a creative workforce, is small; where natural energy has burned out, however, no amount of effort will produce innovation. Recognition of the importance of new projects—even though the business unit itself lacks the resources to exploit them—might help retain the creativity needed in a naturally adaptive organization. Provision of exploitation channels outside the business unit itself—through transfer to other corporate units, new subsidiaries, joint ventures, or entrepreneurial sabbatical leaves—could help the unit's people see the utility of continued idea generation. In a time of diminished general economic growth, no company can afford to reject a good idea because it comes from a unit which is not "supposed to" grow. Neither can we afford to let the "cash cow" label stifle the creativity and adaptability which are vital to survival in increasingly competitive times.

The investment needed to produce creative ideas is small.

The dairying analogy is appropriate for these organizations, so long as we resist the urge to oversimplify it. On the farm, even the best producing cows eventually begin to dry up. The farmer's solution to this is euphemistically called "freshening" the cow: He arranges a date with a bull; she has a calf; the milk begins flowing again. Cloistering the cow—isolating her from everything but the feed trough and the milking machines—assures that she will go dry.

The fault lies not in our stars, but in ourselves . . . .

Consider the "stars." In the BCG model, these are the business units with major shares of growing markets. These are the units which need resources and investments in order to exploit their opportunities. These are the units sought by aggressive, ambitious people, who crave the excitement and challenges of growth. It is in the stars that people blaze career reputations and become recognized as winners.

Unfortunately, however, not all stars turn out to be winners over the long term. Current market share and market growth rates are not sufficient criteria to justify investment, although they suffice to label the business unit as a star. Oversimplification of the BCG prescription can result in investing in situations whose growth rates cannot be sustained in the future for a variety of reasons not apparent in backward scanning market analysis . . . .

Still, with proper qualification, the "star" analogy is appropriate. Think, for example, about the stars themselves. What we know of them is based on old information. When we observe a star through the telescope, we see evidence of an energetic past, but we have no knowledge of whether that same star is still producing energy now. The light we observe has been traveling toward us for eons—billions of years in some cases—and its source may have long since degenerated into a white dwarf or even a black hole, which would absorb any amount of resources we would care to throw at it without ever permitting any return.

Organizational stars, too, take their place in the BCG matrix based on their past performance. Whether they merit additional investment depends on their future potential, not upon their past.

Conclusion

I have no quarrel with the fourth BCG category, the "question mark" business unit. This unit, a nondominant participator in a growing market, requires management thought, says the BCG model. All the categories require management thought.

No management model can safely substitute for analysis and common sense.

No management model can safely substitute for analysis and common sense. Models are useful to managers, to the extent that they can help provide order to the thinking process. Models are dangerous to managers, to the extent that they bias judgment or substitute for analysis . . . .

Source: "Reversing the Images of BCGs Growth/Share Matrix" by John Seeger in the *Strategic Management Journal*, 1984: pp. 93–97, John Wiley & Sons Ltd. Reproduced by permission of John Wiley & Sons Limited.

CHAPTER 5
A VISION OF STRATEGY

"The soul never thinks without a picture."
(Aristotle)

"Small is the number of them that see with their own eyes and feel with their own hearts."
(Albert Einstein)

"You have to be careful if you don't know where you are going, because you might not get there."
(Yogi Berra)

"The reasonable man adapts himself to the world: The unreasonable one persists in trying to adapt the world to himself. Therefore all progress depends on the unreasonable man."
(George Bernard Shaw)

INTRODUCTION TO CHAPTER 5

This chapter is more fun: We're back to flesh-and-blood human beings, really flesh-and-blood individuals—strategic visionaries. Here we had a colorful collection of bytes from which to choose—about strategic visions and strategic visioning, not just strategic visionaries—not to mention lovely quotes (for example, about Mozart seeing a symphony at a glance and Smullyan claiming that the problem begins when something is labeled a problem). Almost all our bytes here are short, in keeping with these word pictures.

Visionaries are easy to find, not like the planners hidden away in offices. The popular business press is littered with the stories of swashbuckling CEOs who have magically guided their companies to huge success (and sometimes later failure). Today we have star CEOs just like we have star athletes. But we wanted something more here; insights to real visions, and real visionaries, sometimes obscure—like the mother of one of us—people who bring exceptional clarity to their strategies, inject new ways of seeing into their businesses, often without fanfare.

We begin with imaging strategy, considering the relationship between a company's images and its strategies. Then we have a look at strategic thinking as seeing, so different from planning and analyzing. But sometimes, as we see next, the visions don't look so good. They can be too abstract, and render their viewers myopic, and so lead organizations astray.

After that, we're on to the visionary—the CEO as "artist," first in reflections of a famous one (Richard Branson), and then at how they differ from craftsmen and technocrats. But must the visionary be heroic? The next bite suggests that just as heroic managers are not visionary, so many effective leaders manage quietly. Finally, we close with a piece by one of us describing what his mother taught him about strategy.

TO SEE OR NOT TO SEE

"When you are inspired by some great purpose, some extraordinary project, all of your thoughts break their bonds; your mind transcends limitations; your consciousness expands in every direction; and you find yourself in a great, new, and wonderful world. Dormant forces, faculties, and talents become alive, and you will discover yourself to be a greater person by far than you ever dreamed yourself to be."

(Yogi Patanjali)

"Sometimes I feel like a rhinoceros who doesn't see well and whose power of concentration is terrible; he charges at something that's a long way off, then forgets where he's going and stops to eat grass."

(Communications executive)

IMAGING STRATEGY
BY HENRY MINTZBERG AND FRANCES WESTLEY

Imagine companies rich in images. Does that make for insightful strategies?

If you think about it, strategy is a "position." But if you *experience* it, strategy is a "perspective." For this word, our dictionary uses phrases such as "depicting spacial relationships," "a mental view," "the state of existing in space before the eye." In other words, strategy making is not only a conceptual, but also a symbolic process, and strategies are bound up with images.

This occurs directly, in the sense that strategies are often conceived, comprehended, and conveyed in terms of metaphors or images. Good strategists are, after all, "visionaries." But this may occur indirectly too, in the link between the strategies pursued by an organization and its more tangible images—its logo, the aesthetics of its products, its architecture, and its internal décor.

Strategies are often conceived and conveyed in terms of metaphors or images.

Can we say that organizations rich in tangible imagery are more inclined to pursue more profound, creative, individualistic strategies, while those poor in such imagery will pursue superficial, banal strategies? Does the name change from the Great Atlantic and Pacific Tea Company to A&P help explain the strategic shift from creative prospecting to fortress defensiveness? Does the redesign of a corporate logo from an elaborate coat of arms (the Royal Bank of Canada in earlier times) or an image rich in symbolism (the horse and rider of the Pony Express) to an abstract, disembodied, stylized logo (the letters *CN* as a single flowing line, or *GM* in a nondescript rectangle) suggest equally abstract, stylized, nondescript strategy (a "generic" position in a well-defined "strategic group," say Burger King in the fast-food hamburger market, as opposed to strategy as the rich and creative interplay of ideas, as in an IKEA)?

When unique, beautiful buildings become uniform glass boxes, when paintings of intricate production facilities are replaced by contemporary abstract art, when "railway" or "telephone" are removed from the corporate name and symbols so that no one can know what the organization produces, does the strategy become as impoverished as the imagery?

Even if the tangible imagery does not influence the strategy per se—if it only reflects it (so to speak) or if both are the victims of some broader process of decay—can we nevertheless reinvigorate strategic vision by reinvigorating that tangible imagery? To enrich strategy, should organizations return to warm architecture, rich logos, names that suggest not just content but style and individuality? *Imagine* the consequences.

Source: Originally published under the title "Spinning on Symbolism: Imaging Strategy" in the *Journal of Management*, Vol. 11, No. 2, 1985: p. 63, Elsevier.

STRATEGIC THINKING AS "SEEING"
BY HENRY MINTZBERG

Maybe we think too much and see too little. What, then, does strategic seeing mean?

I think it best to begin with what I believe strategic thinking is *not*. It is not simply following an "industry recipe," not copying a competitor's strategy or continuing to do what was always done—at least not unless those have been carefully considered choices. In other words, strategic thinking is not mindlessness, nor imitation, nor thoughtless persistence. Nor is it purely cerebral: separating oneself from the subject of one's strategy and working it out ever so cleverly on paper or in a computer, as so much of today's literature urges managers to do.

To me, therefore, strategic thinking differs from ordinary thinking. In fact, because I believe strategic thinkers are appropriately described as "visionaries," I shall characterize the various ingredients of strategic thinking by "seeing" rather than "thinking." I present three pairs of ingredients together with a seventh that knits them altogether into a framework of strategic thinking.

Almost everyone would agree that strategic thinking means *seeing ahead.* ⟶

But in fact, you cannot see ahead unless you can *see behind*, because any good vision of the future has to be rooted in

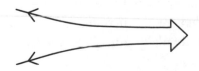

an understanding of the past. To paraphrase Kierkegaard, life may be lived forward, but it is understood backward. That is not to say that strategic thinkers extrapolate the past—I have already argued that they do not do this, at least not mindlessly—but simply that one cannot see the fuure with an ignorance of the past.

Of course, even the best knowledge of the past may not help to see the future. What is key then ... is not to extrapolate trends but to foresee discontinuities. And for that there are not techniques, not much more than informed, creative intuition ....

Many who comment on strategic thinking ... believe that the thinkers should take helicopters. Or at least I assume so because they talk so much about being able to distinguish "the forest from the trees," and the only way I know to do this is to hover well above those trees. To them, therefore, strategic thinking is *seeing above*.

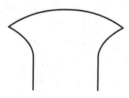
But I wonder if anyone can get the true "big picture" by just seeing above. The forest looks like a rug from a helicopter, and anyone who has taken a walk in one ... knows that forests don't look much like that from the inside. Strategists don't understand much about forests if they stay in helicopters, nor much about organizations if they stay in head offices.

In fact, I prefer another analogy: finding the diamond in the rough. Is that not what strategic thinkers have to do—find the gem of an idea that changes an organization? And that does not come from the big picture at all; it comes from a lot of hard and messy digging. Indeed, there is no big picture (let alone previous gem) readily available to any strategist. Each must construct his or her own—or perhaps I should say paint his or her own—out of the details dug up. Thus, strategic thinking is also

inductive thinking: seeing above must be
supported by *seeing below* . . . .

I believe, however, that you can
see ahead by seeing behind, and see above by
seeing below, and still not be a strategic
thinker. It takes more. For one thing, it
requires creativity. Strategic thinkers see differently from other
people; they pick out the precious gems that others miss. They . . .
challenge conventional wisdom—the industry recipe, the
traditional strategy, the ordinary world perceived by everyone else
who wears blinders—and thereby differentiate their organizations.
Since creative thinking has been referred to as lateral thinking, I
would like to call this *seeing beside* . . . .

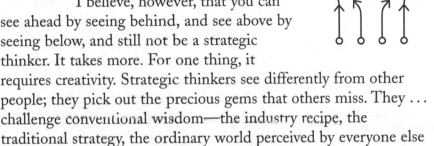

Strategic thinkers see differently from other people; they pick out the precious gems that others miss.

There are many creative ideas in this world, far more
than we can handle—just visit any art gallery. And so to think
strategically requires more than just thinking beside. Those
creative ideas have to be placed into context, to be seen to work in
a world that is to unfold. Strategic thinkers, in other words,
also . . . *see beyond.*

Seeing beyond is different
from seeing ahead. The latter foresees
an expected future by constructing a
framework out of the events of the
past—it intuitively forecasts discontinuities. The former, in
contrast, constructs the future itself—it invents a world that would
not otherwise be . . . .

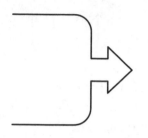

But strategic thinking is not finished yet, for there remains one last necessary ingredient. What is the use of doing all this seeing—ahead and behind, above and below, beside and beyond—if nothing gets done? In other words, for a thinker to deserve the label *strategic*, he or she must also *see* it *through* ...
That can also take systematic planning, to program the consequences of the vision ....
Put this all together and you get the following: strategic thinking as seeing.

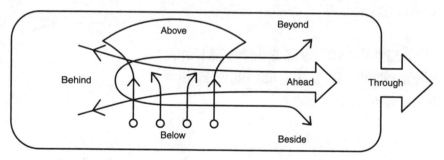

Source: "Strategic Thinking as 'Seeing'" by Henry Mintzberg in J. Nasi, Ed., *Arenas of Strategic Thinking*, Foundation for Economic Education, Helsinki, Finland, 1991.

SEEING A SYMPHONY
MOZART

"First bits and crumbs of the piece come and gradually join together in my mind; then the soul getting warmed to the work, the thing grows more and more, and I spread it out broader and clearer, and at last it gets almost finished in my head, even when it is a long piece, so that I can see the whole of it at a single glance in my mind, as if it were a beautiful painting or a handsome human being; in which way I do not hear it in my imagination at all as a succession—the way it must come later—but all at once as it were. It is a rare feast. All the inventing and making goes on in me as in a beautiful strong dream. But the best of all is the hearing of it all at once."

THE PROBLEM WITH PROBLEMS
SMULLYAN

"Once when I was playing for a musician, he complimented me on the way I played a particular passage. He told me how well I handled a certain modulation and added, 'You don't realize in what a remarkable way you have solved this problem!' I must say, I was thunderstruck ... I was totally unaware of any problem let alone solving one! The whole idea of 'problem solving,' especially in music, strikes me as so weird. Not only weird, but most disharmonious and destructive. Is that how you think of life, as a series of problems to be solved? No wonder you don't enjoy living more than you do! To compliment a musician, or any another artist, on having 'solved problems' to me absolutely is analogous to complimenting the waves of the ocean for solving such a complex system of partial differential equations. Of course, the ocean does its 'waving' in accordance with these differential equations, but it hardly solves them ...."

"I believe my objection to the notion of 'problem' is due to my deep conviction that the moment one labels something as a 'problem' that's when the real problem starts."

"MARKETING MYOPIA" MYOPIA
BY HENRY MINTZBERG

Not all visions are elegant. Those that are ugly are not really a problem—they're plain enough to see. It's the abstract ones that cause the difficulties. They may look interesting, while blinding us to the reality.

In 1960, Theodore Levitt, a marketing professor at the Harvard Business School, published a celebrated article titled "Marketing Myopia." It is difficult to find a manager or planner who does not know the theme, even if he or she has never read the article.

The basic point was that firms should define themselves in terms of broad industry orientation—"underlying generic need" in the words of Kotler and Singh (1981: 39)—rather than narrow product or technology terms. To take Levitt's favorite examples, railroad companies were to see themselves in the transportation business, oil refiners in the energy business.

Companies had a field day with the idea, rushing to redefine themselves in all kinds of fancy ways—for example, the articulated mission of one ball bearing company became "reducing friction." It was even better for the business schools. What better way to stimulate the students than to get them dreaming about how the chicken factory could be in the business of providing human energy, or garbage collection could become beautification? Unfortunately, it was all too easy, a cerebral exercise that, while opening vistas, could also detach people from the mundane world of plucking and compacting.

Often the problem came down to some awfully ambitious assumptions about the strategic capabilities of an organization—namely that these are almost limitless, or at least very adaptable. Thus we have the example from George Steiner (1979), presented in apparent seriousness, that "buggy whip manufacturers might still be around if they had said their business was not making buggy whips but self-starters for carriages." But what in the world would have made them capable of doing that? These two products shared nothing in common—no material supply, no technology, no production process, no distribution channel—save a thought in somebody's head about making vehicles move. Why should starters have been any more of a logical product diversification for them than, say, fan belts or the pumping of gas? As Heller suggested, "instead of being in transportation accessories or guidance systems," why could the buggy whip manufacturers not have defined their business as "flagellation?" (quoted in Normann, 1977: 34).

Why should a few clever words on a piece of paper enable a railroad company to fly airplanes, or for that matter run taxicabs? Levitt wrote that "once it genuinely thinks of its business as taking care of people's transportation needs, nothing can stop it from creating its own extravagantly profitable growth" (1960: 53)—nothing except the limitations of its own distinctive competences. Words on paper do not transform a company.

Words on paper do not transform a company.

Levitt's intention was to broaden the vision of managers. At that he may have succeeded—all too well. As Kotler and Singh, also from marketing, argued: "very little in the world . . . is not potentially the energy business" (1981: 34). Ironically, by in effect redefining strategy from position to perspective, Levitt really *reduced* its breadth. Internal capability got lost; only the market opportunity mattered. Products did not count (railroad executives defined their industry "wrong" because "they were product-oriented instead of consumer-oriented" [p. 45]), nor did production ("the particular form of manufacturing, processing, or what-have-you cannot be considered as a vital aspect of the industry" [p. 55]). But what makes market intrinsically more important than product or production, or, for that matter, a smart researcher in the laboratory? Organizations have to build on whatever strengths they can make use of, while they must avoid being submerged by weaknesses that they may have never considered, marketing ones included.

Critics of Levitt's article have had their own field day with the terminology, pointing out the dangers of "marketing hyperopia," where "vision is better for distant than for near objects" (Kotler and Singh, 1981: 39), or of "marketing macropia," which escalates previously narrow market segments "beyond experience or prudence" (Baughman, 1974: 65). I prefer to conclude simply that Levitt's notion of marketing myopia itself proved myopic.

Source: *The Rise and Fall of Strategic Planning* by Henry Mintzberg, New York: Free Press, 1994: pp. 279–281.

References
Baughman, J.P. (1974) *Problems and Performance of the Role of the Chief Executive in the General Electric Company, 1882–1974*, working paper Graduate School of Business Administration, Harvard University.

Kotler, P. and Singh, R. (1981) "Marketing Warfare in the 1980s," *Journal of Business Strategy*, Winter, 1981, pp. 30–41.

Levitt, T. (1960) "Marketing Myopia," *Harvard Business Review*, July/August, 1960, pp. 45–56.

Normann, R. (1977) *Management for Growth*, New York: Wiley.

Steiner, G.A. (1979) *Strategic Planning; What Every Manager Must Know*, New York: Free Press.

RECOGNIZING THE CEO AS ARTIST
BY PATRICIA PITCHER

Pat Pitcher of the *École des hautes études commerciales* of Montreal has written a fascinating book about managers as artists, craftsmen, and technocrats. In this short passage, she describes the artists.

How do you recognize artists? ... What is your strategic plan for the future? Answer: "to get big," "to hit $5 billion in sales," "to beat the pants off the competition," "to be a world leader by 2020." Artists may be a little short on the details, on the how. Board presentations are sometimes a little loose—unless they are done by the chief financial officer. The artist CEO might get overtly angry or euphoric at board meetings. How does the artist CEO talk? Listen to one.

> *What is strategy anyway? Grand plan? No. You try to instill a vision you have and get people to buy in. The strategy comes from astrology; quirks, dreams, love affairs, science fiction, perception of society, some madness probably, ability to guess. It is clear but fluid. Action brings precision. Very vague, but becomes clear in the act of transformation. Creation is the storm.*

Strategy comes from astrology; quirks, dreams, love affairs, science fiction, perception of society, some madness probably, ability to guess.

When CEOs like this talk to their boards about "astrology; quirks, dreams," boards have a tendency to get a little uneasy. This person's peers and colleagues describe him or her as bold, daring, exciting, volatile, intuitive, entrepreneurial, inspiring, imaginative, unpredictable, and funny. Technocrats will apply [to them] labels like "Star-Trekky", or more simply, nuts. The artist makes both fast friends and abiding enemies. Very few have a neutral reaction. The organization as a whole is an exciting place to be; confusing maybe, dizzying maybe, but exciting nonetheless.

Source: From the article originally titled "Balancing Personality Types at the Top" in *Business Quarterly*, Winter, 1993 published by the Western Business School, University of Western Ontario, London, Canada.

REFLECTIONS OF AN ENTREPRENEUR
BY RICHARD BRANSON

Richard Branson is certainly a famous entrepreneur, what with all his Virgin enterprises. Here's his advice:

> "The biggest risk any of us can take is to invest money in a business that we don't know. Very few of the businesses that Virgin has set up have been in completely new fields."

> "I have not depended on others to do surveys or market research, or to develop grand strategies. I have taken the view that the risk to the company is best reduced by my own involvement in the nitty-gritty of the new business."

> " ... There is always another deal. Deals are like London buses—there's always another one coming along."

> " ... Reduce the scale of ... risk through joint ventures ... [and] have a way out of a high-risk venture."

> " ... As businesses grow, watch out for management losing touch with the basics—normally the customer."

> "[Our] 'keep it small' rule enables ... more than usual numbers of managers the challenge and excitement of running their own businesses."

> " ... Pursue a 'buy, don't make' strategy."

> "Having evaluated an investment ... and having decided to make an investment, don't pussyfoot around. Go for it!"

Source: "Reflections of a Risk Taker" by Richard Branson in the *McKinsey Quarterly*, Summer, 1986: pp. 13–18.

ENTREPRENEURSHIP AND PLANNING
BY AMAR BHIDE

If what Amar Bhide of the Columbia University School of Business has to say here about successful entrepreneurship and the practice of planning is true, then why do we demand all those business plans of entrepreneurs?

Interviews with the founders of 100 companies on the 1989 *Inc.* "500" list of the fastest-growing companies in the United States revealed that entrepreneurs spent little effort on their initial business plan:

> 41 percent had no business plan at all.
> 26 percent had just a rudimentary, back-of-the-envelope type of plan.
> 5 percent worked up financial projections for investors.
> 28 percent wrote up a full-blown plan.

Many entrepreneurs, the interview suggested, don't bother with well-formulated plans for good reasons. They thrive in rapidly changing industries and niches that tend to deter established companies. And under these fluid conditions, an ability to roll with the punches is much more important than careful planning ....

Peter [Zacharkiw] did not conduct any research ... He placed an ad in the *Washington Post* to sell his computer. He got over 50 responses and sold his machine for a profit. Peter figured that if he had had 50 machines, he could have sold them all and decided to begin selling computers from his home ... "First, we sold to individuals responding to ads. But these people were working for companies, and they would tell their purchasing agents, 'Hey, I know where you can get these.' It was an all-referral business. I gave better service than anyone else" ... After customers started asking for Compaq machines, [his firm] became a Compaq dealer, and the business really took off. "We're very reactive, not proactive," Peter observes. "Business comes to us, and we react. I've never had a business plan."

Source: Reprinted by permission of *Harvard Business Review* from "The Entrepreneur's Craft Strategies That Work" by Amar Bhide, March–April 1994. Copyright © by The Harvard Business School Publishing Corporation; all rights reserved.

MANAGING QUIETLY
BY HENRY MINTZBERG

Vision can be quiet—indeed, in the sense of the metaphor, it always is. So maybe some effective visionaries manage not so much heroically as quietly.

A prominent business magazine hires a journalist to write about the chief executive of a major corporation. The man has been at the helm for several years and is considered highly effective. The journalist submits an excellent piece, capturing the very spirit of the man's managerial style. The magazine rejects it—not exciting enough, no hype. Yet the company has just broken profit records for its industry.

Not far away, another major corporation is undergoing dramatic transformation. Change is everywhere, the place is teeming with consultants, people are being released in huge numbers. The chief executive has been all over the business press. Suddenly he is fired: the board considers the turnaround a failure.

Go back 5, 10, 20 or more years and read the business press—about John Scully at Apple, James Robinson at American Express, Robert McNamara at the Defense Department. Heroes of American management all ... for a time. Then consider this proposition: Maybe really good management is boring. Maybe the press is the problem, alongside the so-called gurus, since they are the ones who personalize success and deify the leaders (before they defile them). After all, corporations are large and complicated; it takes a lot of effort to find out what has really

Maybe really good management is boring.

been going on. It is much easier to assume that the great one did it all. Makes for better stories too.

"Forget what you know about how business should work—most of it is wrong!" screams the cover of that book called *Reengineering the Corporation* (by Hammer and Champy, 1993). Just like that. "Business reengineering means putting aside much of the received wisdom of two hundred years of industrial management," say the authors. Never mind that Henry Ford and Frederick Taylor, to name just two, "reengineered" businesses nearly a century ago. The new brand of reengineering "is to the next revolution of business what the specialization of labor was to the last" (meaning the Industrial Revolution). Are we so numbed by the hype of management that we accept such overstatement as normal? There is no shortage of noisy words in the field of management. A few favored standbys merit special comment:

> *Globalization*: The Red Cross Federation headquarters in Geneva, Switzerland, has managers from over 50 countries. Few are Swiss, not the secretary general nor the three under secretary generals. The closest I know to a global company is perhaps Royal Dutch Shell, most of whose senior management comes from two countries—twice as many as almost any other company I can think of. But still a long way from the Red Cross Federation. Global coverage does not mean a global mind-set.

> *Shareholder value*: Is "shareholder value" just another old way to sell the future cheap? Is this just an easy way for chief executives without ideas to squeeze money out of rich corporations?

> *Empowerment*: Organizations that have real empowerment don't talk about it. Those that make a lot of noise about it generally lack it: They have been

spending too much of their past disempowering everybody. Then, suddenly, empowerment appears as a gift from the gods. In actual fact, real empowerment is a most natural state of affairs: people know what they have to do and simply get on with it, like the worker bees in a beehive.

> *Change management*: This is the ultimate in managerial noise. Companies are being turned around left and right—all part of today's managerial correctness, which, in its mindlessness, puts political correctness to shame.

On March 2, 1998, *Fortune* put on display "America's Most Admired Corporations." But the accompanying article said hardly anything about these corporations. It was all about their leaders. After all, if the corporations succeeded, it must have been the bosses. "There is, believe it or not, some academic literature that suggests that leadership doesn't matter," we are told by the astonished *Fortune* writer. Well, this academic is no less astonished: There are, believe it or not, some business magazines so mesmerized with leadership that nothing else matters. "In four years Gerstner has added more than $40 billion to IBM's share value," this magazine once proclaimed. All by himself!

Years ago, Peter Drucker wrote that the administrator works within the constraints; the manager removes the constraints. Later, Abraham Zaleznik claimed that managers merely manage; real leaders lead. Now we seem to be moving beyond leaders who merely lead; today heroes save. Soon heroes will only save; then gods will redeem.

Let's go back to that book on reengineering, the same page quoted earlier: "What matters in reengineering is how we want to organize work *today*, given the demands of *today's* market and the power of *today's* technologies. How people and companies did things yesterday doesn't matter to the business reengineer" (italics added).

Today, today, always today. But if you want the imagination to see the future, then you'd better have the wisdom to appreciate the past. Show me a chief executive who ignores yesterday, who favors the new outsider over the experienced insider, the quick fix over steady progress, and I'll show you a chief executive who is destroying an organization.

If you want the imagination to see the future, then you'd better have the wisdom to appreciate the past.

To "turn around" is to end up facing the same way. Maybe that is the problem: all this turning around. Might not the white knight of management be the black holes of organizations? What good is the great leader if everything collapses when he or she leaves? Perhaps good companies don't need to be turned around at all because they are not constantly being thrust into crises by leaders who have to make their marks today. Maybe these companies are simply managed quietly.

To "turn around" is to end up facing the same way. Maybe that is the problem: all this turning around. Might not the white knight of management be the black holes of organizations?

What has been the greatest advance ever in health care? Not the dramatic discoveries of penicillin or insulin, it has been argued, but simply cleaning up the water supply. Perhaps, then, it is time to clean up our organizations, as well as our thinking. In this spirit I offer a few thoughts about some of the quiet words of managing.

> *Inspiring*: Quiet managers don't empower their people. They *inspire* them. They create the conditions that foster openness and release energy. The queen bee, for example, does not make decisions; she just emits a chemical substance that holds the whole social system together. In human hives, that is called culture.

Quiet managers strengthen the cultural bonds between people, not by treating them as detachable "human resources," but as respected members of a cohesive social system. When people are trusted, they do not have to be empowered.

The queen bee does not take credit for the worker bees' doing their jobs effectively. She just does her job effectively, so that they can do theirs. There are no bonuses for the queen bee beyond what she needs.

> *Caring*: Quiet managers care for their organizations; they do not try to slice away problems as surgeons do. They spend more time preventing problems than fixing them. It is like the best of nursing: gentle care that, in itself, becomes cure.

> *Infusing*: "If you want to know what problems we have encountered over the years," someone from a major airline once told me, "just look at our headquarters units. Every time we have a problem, we create a new unit to deal with it." That is management by intrusion. Stick in someone or something to fix it.

Quiet managing is about *infusion*, change that seeps in slowly, steadily, profoundly. Rather than having change thrust upon them in dramatic, superficial episodes, everyone takes responsibility for making sure that serious changes take hold. To achieve this there is no substitute for a leadership with an intimate understanding of the organization working with a workforce that is respected and trusted.

> *Initiating*: Moses supplies our image of the strategy process: walking down the mountain carrying the word from on high to the waiting faithful. Redemption from the heavens. Of course, there are too many people to read the tablets, so the leaders have to shout these "formulations" to all these "implementors." All so very neat.

Except that life in the valleys below is rich and complicated. And that is what strategy has to be about—not the neat abstractions of the executive suite, but the messy patterns of daily life. So long as loud management stays up there disconnected, it can shout down all the strategies it likes: They will never work.

Quiet management is about rolling up sleeves and finding out what is going on. And it is not parachuted down on the organization; it rises up from the base. But it never leaves that base. It functions "on the floor," where the knowledge for strategy making lies. Such management blends into the daily life of the corporation, so that all sorts of people with their feet planted firmly on the ground can pursue exciting initiatives. Then managers who are in touch with them can champion these initiatives and so stimulate the process by which strategies evolve.

Quiet managing functions "on the floor" where the knowledge for strategy making lies.

Put differently, the manager is not the organization any more than a painting of a pipe is a pipe. The healthy organization does not leap from one hero to another; it is a collective social system that naturally survives changes in leadership.

Quiet management is about thoughtfulness rooted in experience. Words like *wisdom*, *trust*, *dedication*, and *judgment* apply. Leadership works because it is legitimate, meaning that it is an integral part of the organization and so has the respect of everyone there. Tomorrow is appreciated because yesterday is honored. That makes today a pleasure. Indeed, the best managing of all may well be silent. That way people can say, "We did it ourselves." Because we did.

Source: Reprinted in excerpted form from "Managing Quietly" by H. Mintzberg in *Leader to Leader*, Spring, 1999: pp. 24–30.

Reference
Hammer, M. and Champy, J. (1993) *Reengineering the Corporation*, New York: HarperCollins.

WHAT MY MOTHER TAUGHT ME ABOUT STRATEGY
BY JOSEPH LAMPEL

Joe found many of the bytes and bites in this book, digging them up in all kinds of wild and wooly places. But we, his two co-authors, did not expect this one—from his wild and wooly heart. And it captures the spirit of the visionary entrepreneur so charmingly. How better to end this chapter!

Strategy was once chiefly practice, but with a dash of theory. Then academics got into the act and strategy became an intellectual activity. Gradually the bright lights of theory began to outshine the mundane business of making strategy happen in practice. Fashionable theories brought ready-made solutions to managers beset by uncertainty. And though everyone admitted that practice is the ultimate test of theory, all too often reality was filtered—by data collection and by the machinery of analysis.

Reality, however, has a way of sneaking in when you least expect it. I certainly did not expect my own mother to teach me about the limits of theory in strategy. That she did says as much about the role that old-fashioned values such as perseverance and ingenuity play in strategy, as it does about how easy it is for theory to ignore the power of individuals to go against received wisdom.

The story, or rather my lesson, begins soon after my mother opened a new boutique in Alberta's famous "West Edmonton Mall." I was in the midst of my doctoral studies in strategic management and needed a break. So I flew over to see my parents, but also to see my mother's new store. This was by no means her first boutique. The location, however, certainly marked this one as her most ambitious. Dubbed by the *Guinness Book of Records* as the world's largest shopping mall, the West Edmonton is certainly colossal. In addition to 800 stores, it boasts an amusement park, a hotel, a waterpark, and an indoor lake with a functioning submarine. My mother's modest boutique occupied a tiny corner in this sprawling retail and entertainment complex. Located near one of the mall's 58 entrances, it sold women's wear and assorted gifts, all imported from the Far East.

Being small in the world's largest mall did not faze my mother. Indeed, it had the opposite effect. On the second day of my visit, she showed me the monthly sales reports put out by the mall's management. It listed the top 20 stores by order of sales per square foot. The top earner received special mention, and had a place of pride in the mall's competitive hierarchy. In the month preceding my visit the top position was occupied by Sears—a position that the giant department store enjoyed frequently. My mother pointed this out, and then declared with confidence: "This is what I intend to do. One day I will beat Sears and make it to the top of the list."

Looking closely at the list, I noted that the top sellers were the large department stores like Sears, the Bay, and Zellers. The disparity between the reality of these giants and my mother's ambition was not only disconcerting, more to the point it also flew in the face of the readings in which I was engrossed at the time. The work of Michael Porter in particular made fashionable the idea that competitors cluster into "strategic groups" according to their strategic profile. Large department stores therefore belonged in a single group because they competed with other large department stores. Small specialist boutiques like my mother's belonged in a different group because they competed with other small boutiques. It made no sense for firms from one group to compete with firms from the other. The large department stores offered low prices and shopping convenience, and the small boutiques offered specialized product line and personal service. The department stores dominated by virtue of scale and scope, the small boutiques survived by nurturing niches that were of little interest to the merchandising giants.

I tried to explain all this to my mother. She would have none of it. Being number one in the West Edmonton meant more to her than my closely reasoned arguments. She respected my knowledge of strategy (or more precisely my knowledge of strategy theory), but she was stubbornly set on chasing the dream of seeing her name at the top of the list.

I flew back to Montreal with a sense of foreboding. There was no question that my mother was a good businesswoman, but it did not escape my notice that a high proportion of the small stores in the West Edmonton were either closed, or going out of business. Competition for customers in the West Edmonton mall was fierce. With so many stores in the same location it was not surprising that many went to the wall, but in addition the oil boom of the 1970s was giving way to the economic doldrums of the eighties. The omens did not look good.

My mother, however, did not bother with environmental analysis. She was far too busy running the store. For her, being in business did not mean simply opening the store and waiting for the customers to come in. For her a store was a living system that required constant tending. She regularly

My mother, however, did not bother with environmental analysis. She was far too busy running the store.

rearranged the window display, moved popular merchandise to the front, put slow-moving merchandise on sale. She was always ready with a smile and hello for browsing customers, a cup of coffee for those who tried on a skirt or a dress, and a chair for the spouse or boyfriend while they made up their mind. A skilled seamstress, she made alterations for free. And instead of returning merchandise that was damaged in transit, she got a substantial refund from the supplier and fixed the merchandise herself.

Periodically, she flew to Toronto to visit her suppliers. They would often send a car to pick her up at the airport. She paid upfront for her merchandise, but she bargained hard— offering to flip a coin when the negotiations came down to a difference of a couple of dollars per unit. Amazingly, the supplier on the spot usually agreed.

Six months after my visit she called with the news: After climbing steadily in the ranking, her boutique was listed as the store generating the most sales per square foot for that month. Congratulations came from every quarter. She was particularly pleased when the manager of the Sears store came in person to congratulate her. She knew better than to suppose that her position at the top was sustainable, but she basked in the limelight while it lasted.

Later that month I underwent my doctoral qualifying examination in strategic management. The panel approved of my knowledge of the research literature, and judged my skills at developing theory to be sufficiently promising. Porter and strategic groups came up, and I made the appropriate comments but I did not mention my mother's little store. For by then I had learned that practice in the academe is an invited guest; it must be on the approved list, and if it shows up it must be on its best behavior. My mother was too much of a strategic anarchist to make it on the list, and she certainly would not have been on her best behavior.

CHAPTER 6
INSIDE THE STRATEGIST'S HEAD

"Knowing others is intelligence; knowing yourself is true wisdom."
[Lao Tse]

"I'll see it when I believe it."

"It is in a country unfamiliar emotionally and topographically that one needs poems and roadmaps."
[Clifford Geertz]

INTRODUCTION TO CHAPTER 6

Get a can opener and pry inside the cavity of the human brain. What do you see? If you did this quite literally, you wouldn't see much at all. Cognitive psychologists and others who do this, not quite so literally, don't see much at all either. But they do see some things, and we try to capture some of that here, for how are we to appreciate strategy if we can't pry into the head of the strategist?

We know a bit, for example, about the mental models, or "maps," that people try to use in processes like strategy making; we also know about the many distortions exhibited by decision makers of all kinds. What we don't know so much about is where the great ideas come from, and how people synthesize what they know to "attain concepts"—a fancy term for creating strategies.

We begin with a short excerpt on the biases and limitations of human judgment. Then we get into the biases and limitations of animal judgment—pigeons and fish, to be specific. They can be awfully like us.

But it is not all biases and limitations, not for them any more than for us. So we go next to the zoo, where Jeanne Liedtka, who brought us the "little black dress," found out how much the orangutans can teach us about strategic thinking.

Games can do that too. Push people to the limit—put them up against a real opponent, namely a computer, and in a real game of strategy, namely chess, or so it seems—and watch what you find out. Fascinating stuff in the next byte.

Our last two are bites about plain old people stripped of their fancy adornments. One is a famous old fable about the emperor who was sold a bill of goods, so to speak, by a couple of swindlers. Ego plays a role in strategy too. The other is about a company called Enron. We leave you to make the connection.

BIASES AND LIMITATIONS OF JUDGMENT: HUMANS
BY SPYROS G. MAKRIDAKIS

Scholars have long been fascinated by the peculiarities of how we "process information," especially the biases and distortions we exhibit. Spyros Makridakis, a leading authority in forecasting and professor at Insead, demonstrates, rather depressingly, how our decisions are plagued by an array of biases.

In this [article], I provide what cognitive psychologists call disconfirming evidence, since it probably goes contrary to common opinions and beliefs. Strong empirical evidence shows that an [article] like this is less likely to be sought out and read. Furthermore, once it has been read, it is unlikely that the arguments will cause much changing of minds. On the contrary, people are more likely to select and read [something] that supports their current opinions or beliefs and does not require changing their minds. Here is some concrete information about what I am describing: supportive and disconfirming evidence.

       Wason (1972), a cognitive psychologist, made it his life's goal to learn more about how people search for information and evidence. He found that as much as 90 percent of all the information we are searching for aims at supporting views, beliefs, or hypotheses that we have long cherished. Thus, if a manager thinks that a certain promotional campaign will increase his sales

90 percent of all the information we are searching for aims at supporting views, beliefs, or hypotheses that we have long cherished.

he will look for supportive evidence to prove that the belief (or, more precisely, hypothesis) is correct. Unfortunately, however, it is practically impossible to prove the hypothesis that the promotional campaign is effective simply by observing that sales go up, for there are many factors other than promotions that can cause sales to rise. In this case, supportive evidence can *never* prove the hypothesis is right. That could be done by stopping the promotional campaign for a period of time, the equivalent of getting disconfirming evidence. If the sales then go down, the hypothesis can be proved to be right. If the campaign is stopped several times in several regions, and the outcome is always the same, it can then be ascertained with confidence that the decrease in sales is not due to chance but is influenced by the decrease in advertising. Although it might be impractical to stop promotions or advertising, from a scientific view it is the only way to prove, beyond any reasonable doubt, that the hypothesis that promotions increase sales is correct. People, however, do not look for disconfirming evidence . . . .

There is another side to the picture. We tend to remember information that confirms our beliefs far better than information that disproves them. In experiments, believers have tended to remember confirming material with 100 percent accuracy, but negative material only about 40 percent of the time. Skeptics, on the other hand, have remembered both supportive and disconfirming evidence equally well—their accuracy was 90 percent in both cases. Thus, not only do we search for supportive evidence, but once we find it we tend to remember it more accurately . . . .

The higher up a manager is in the organization, the more the information he or she receives is filtered by several levels of subordinates, as assistants, and secretaries. They know, or think they do, what the manager wants to hear and selectively present supportive information . . . .

Can biases be avoided if decisions are made in groups? Unfortunately not—in fact there is evidence suggesting that groups amplify bias by introducing groupthink (a phenomenon that develops when group members become supportive of their leader and each other, thus avoiding conflict and dissent during their meetings) . . . .

Another type of judgmental bias that can threaten the effectiveness of decision making is that of unfounded beliefs or conventional wisdom. We have grown up in a culture where we accept certain statements as true, though they may not be. For instance, we believe that the more information we have, the more accurate our decisions will be. Empirical evidence does not support such a belief. Instead, more information merely seems to increase our confidence that we are right without necessarily improving the accuracy of our decisions . . . .

If a manager accepts the human biases I have described in this [article], he cannot assume rationality from his subordinates, superiors, or competitors. This complicates matters considerably, as all economic theories and the vast majority of managerial ones assume cold rationality. How, for instance, does a manager deal with a competitor who is driven by irrational motives? He cannot understand them or predict how they will influence the competitor's decisions. There is no way of doing so, since irrationality cannot be predicted. Thus, another challenge facing managers is to accept the possibility of irrationality and attempt to rationalize it. That is probably the hardest of all challenges a manager must face. Worse, the lack of rationality is not limited to competitors only but exists everywhere. Jealousy, excessive ambition, fighting for no apparent reason, breakdowns in communication, and similar irrational behavior abound in any organization and must be dealt with in a sensible manner in order to neutralize or reduce their negative effects as far as is possible. The challenge is considerable, but it is one that must be confronted. We must move forward, although we know the road will not always be smooth.

Source: Reprinted and edited with the permission of The Free Press, a Division of Simon & Schuster Adult Publishing Group, from *Forecasting, Planning, and Strategy for the 21st Century* by Spyros G. Makridakis. Copyright © 1990 by Spyros G. Makridakis. All rights reserved.

Reference
Wason, P. C. and Johnson-Laird P. N. (1972) *Psychology of Reasoning: Structure and Content*, London: Batsford.

BIASES AND LIMITATIONS OF JUDGMENT: ANIMALS

The pigeon

"Suppose we give a pigeon a small amount of food every 15 seconds regardless of what he is doing. When the food is first given the pigeon will be behaving in some way—if only standing still—and conditioning will take place. It is then more probable that the same behavior will be in progress when the food is given again. If this proves to be the case, the 'operant' will be further strengthened. If not, some other behavior reaches a frequency at which it is often reinforced. It then becomes a permanent part of the repertoire of the bird even though the food has been given by a clock which is unrelated to the bird's behavior. Conspicuous responses which have been established in this way include turning sharply to one side, hopping from one foot to the other and back, bowing and scraping, turning around, strutting, and raising the head."

(Skinner)

The pike

"Most readers will be familiar with the so-called pike syndrome. If you put a pike in a tank and put in a handful of minnows, the pike will watch them for a while and when it's hungry will eat them. If you then put a sheet of clear glass in the tank, with the pike on one side and the minnows on the other, the pike will try to eat the minnows, and will continue to try for several hours before giving up. If you then take the glass out, the fish will all swim around together and the pike, conditioned not to attack the minnows, will starve to death."

(Unknown)

EVERYTHING I NEED TO KNOW ABOUT STRATEGY I LEARNED AT THE NATIONAL ZOO
BY JEANNE LIEDTKA

Jeanne Liedtka, who probably does not visit zoos in a little black dress, may have more to say about how strategists should think than anyone else. That is because she learned it from the orangutans.

It was elementary school field trip day at the National Zoo, and the lines at the animal exhibits were long and hot. Escaping to the deserted orangutan learning laboratory, called the ThinkTank, I was intrigued to find an exhibit titled "Can Animals Think?" The scientists, I learned, used only three criteria to determine the existence of thinking in this simian world: (1) the evidence of ability to create and hold in mind an image, a mental representation of something not present; (2) the evidence of intention, having a goal or purpose and a plan to achieve that purpose in a certain way; and (3) the evidence of flexibility, the ability to discover multiple ways to reach a goal when the initial plan failed to work. Image, intention, flexibility. How many of the managers and MBAs I work with, I wondered, could pass the orangutan test?

Strategic planning is either dead or rising again, depending upon how you define the practice. Regardless, traditional strategic planning approaches—and their failed promise—have been the favored scapegoat among leading thinkers in the strategy field for several years. Formal planning breeds bureaucracy and myopia, not curiosity and creativity. It tends to inhibit, rather than support, significant change. It wrests power from employees closest to the customer, the ones who know the business, and gives it to those at the top of the hierarchy and their henchmen, who deal in analysis and work in isolation. The demise of traditional strategic planning is so well accepted that to discuss it seems to risk proverbially beating a dead horse. As we put aside 35 or so years worth of writings on the subject, the only question of interest seems to be "What's next?"

Strategic thinking, of course. Again, the chorus of voices speak in unison. Strategic thinking breeds inventiveness and innovation. It engenders speed and flexibility. It invites employees at all levels into the strategic conversation and engages them as a result. At this high altitude level of discussion, the promise of strategic thinking is as clear to us as are the pitfalls of planning.

But what remains less clear amid the hoopla is what strategic thinking consists of, or what it looks like in practice. What is clear is that it probably will not be easy. Sure, if we define "strategic thinking" as "thinking about strategy," that won't seem too tough for an article on competition from the chief executive in the company newsletter, a few more suggestion boxes on the factory floor, maybe even a "town meeting" to kick off the annual budget process, and we're on our way. We can handle that. Will that get us to the promised land of innovative, responsive, and efficient organizations? "As if," to quote my teenage daughter. Let's put managers and MBAs to the orangutan test.

Although all of these are good ideas, they don't come close to building a capability for real strategic thinking. To understand what that looked like in practice, I needed to spend the day at the zoo.

The three tests: image, intention, flexibility. It sounded so simple. The more I thought about it, the more I became convinced that those orangutans had cracked the code. Really, what more did you need to say to understand strategic thinking?

Test 1: Image
Strategic thinkers hold in mind an image, a mental representation of something not currently present. Whether we call that image the organization's strategic intent (à la Hamel and Prahalad), or vision (à la Porris and Collins), or model of the business (à la Drucker) really doesn't matter; what counts is what's in it. To think about strategy well, that image must contain a rich understanding of the larger context in which the organization operates today, along with the dynamics of that context.

For a long time, strategy was viewed solely in an industry-based context, and within that context the dynamic worth paying attention to was rivalry within the industry. As the boundaries between industries have begun to dissolve, a broader view has become necessary. New voices, like Jim Moore, have begun to argue that we must move beyond industry to an "ecosystem" perspective, to use Moore's term. Here, we see the organization as part of a larger network of suppliers, working cooperatively to forge a system that creates value for customers throughout the process—and competing against other end-to-end ecosystems to see who can best meet customer needs. This broader concept of context is fundamental to sound strategic thinking.

Such issues as bargaining power are no less important than they were in the old world—but they need to be reframed, because many of our old categories no longer work. The point is that we need to develop more sophisticated ways to look at our increasingly messy world. And that "we" includes a lot more people than it used to, many of whom have been told for a long time that their job is not to think, but to do what they are told.

Equally essential to strategic thinking is the understanding of the internal system, and the interdependencies it contains. Experience shows that optimizing individual parts of a larger system does not usually optimize the system as a whole. Success in the world of the future requires an ability to continuously redesign what we do. That rests on the ability to visualize the larger system of which we are a part.

As a case in point, look at health care. I spend a lot of time talking to doctors, most of whom are really committed to doing their best for their patients. I work with two clinics: One takes a patient with a suspicious lump from initial screening to biopsy and test results all in less than four hours; the second one takes almost two weeks. Pretty obvious quality difference there. Do the docs in the second clinic believe they are providing inferior care? Absolutely not, and they'd be insulted if you suggested that they didn't care about quality.

Real breakthroughs in quality and efficiency happen when everybody in the system sees the big picture and works toward the best results at that level, even if it means downplaying their role. But visualizing today's system is not enough. We also need a vivid image of the future system we want to create. Twenty years of writing and research on the subject of change have already made that point: We know that our ability to change depends heavily on the clarity of the future image we are working toward—the mental representation of what doesn't exist today. The gap between today's reality and tomorrow's vision drives strategic intent, we've been told.

Strategic thinkers, then, see today's systems and understand the interdependencies among their parts. Beyond that,

Our ability to change depends heavily on the clarity of the future image we are working toward.

they see an image of tomorrow's desired new system and the likely path that today's system must follow in order to evolve into tomorrow's. Without such new ways of seeing, how can we hope to discover and employ new ways of behaving?

Test 1 for orangutans, then, seems to work just as well for us humans.

Test 2: Intention

Truth be told, some of us humans have gotten pretty good at the image part. Just pick up any annual report. The tricky part is making the leap from seeing to behaving. The orangutans had an answer for this too: the role of intention. Strategic thinking has to involve linking the future image of the organization with the personal choices I make, in my role within the larger system. It also means caring about whether that image materializes, and channeling my efforts accordingly. For me, the quintessential lesson on this point comes out of a two-minute segment in an old Tom Peters' *In Search of Excellence* video. In it, a street sweeper at Disney World is working with a new trainee. As they walk down the streets of the Magic Kingdom with their brooms and pans, sweeping cigarette butts as they walk, the experienced hand tells the new trainee, "You're going to get interrupted with a lot of questions from the guests. And even though you get asked the same question over and over again, you need to remember that, for each of them, it's the first time they've asked it."

In the strategy field, we have devoted an enormous amount of time to talking about the "three levels" of strategy: corporate, business, and function. But we've ignored the most important level of all: the personal. Levels one, two, and three, we are told, ask the important questions: "What businesses are we in?" "How do we compete within each business?" and "What does that mean for each functional area?" Level four, I would argue, asks the ultimate question: "What does this mean for me—what is my role in making that other stuff happen?"

When that question is answered with clarity and consistency, as it has been for the Disney street sweeper, the image starts to mean more than the laminated plastic aphorism in my wallet or on my office wall. Back that up with structures, information, and reward systems that support it, and meaningful change becomes a real possibility.

Forget about oil, capital, and systems programmers who understand your business—I'd argue that attention is the scarcest resource in business today. We've got too much information, too many change initiatives, too many e-mails, and it's only going to get worse. Many organizations today really ought to carry this label.

No wonder Dilbert has spawned its own growth industry. Psychologists argue that attention is "psychic energy." Psychic energy is essential to innovation and creativity, and to growth and development of the human mind itself. The same is true for organizations. Without focus, the risks of dissipating and squandering the psychic energy of employees is great. If I'm not able to make sense out of my role in the big picture and channel my efforts accordingly, nothing much happens.

I also need to care about the goal. The idea that strategic thinking might have an emotional overtone is shocking, indeed, but remember that we're using the orangutan's test. Caring invokes a new question beyond "What are we doing?" to "Why are we doing it?" When we add caring to seeing, we add intention to image, and we add purpose to plans.

I wasn't sure how the animal scientists figured all this out in the orangutan world, but I concluded that Test 2 was right on target for business. Strategic thinking involved translating a high-altitude image into a more personal purpose and investing energy into making the day-to-day choices that supported that purpose.

Test 3: Flexibility

Based on what I'd learned from the first two tests alone, I was ready to call my day at the zoo worthwhile. But the best was yet to come, because Test 3 filled in the final missing piece in the puzzle called "strategic thinking"—evidence of flexibility. Initially, I found Test 3 disconcerting. You mean, after we create this richly detailed, systems view of our world, understand how it all fits together, and commit ourselves to a role in making it happen, we have to be open to changing it? This seemed so unfair. How could people be committed to a purpose and be flexible at the same time? I was beginning to lose faith that we could ever hope to meet their third test.

How could people be committed to a purpose and be flexible at the same time?

Fortunately, a group of fourth graders entered the learning lab as I was struggling with Test 3, and offered to help me. They quickly diagnosed that I was being hindered by a common adult malady—I was convinced that once you had finished thinking about something, you moved on to doing it and never looked back. Life doesn't work that way, the fourth graders explained. Learning, not knowing, was the key to success. And flexibility depended on the capacity to learn continuously. This rang a bell with a lot of talk about "learning organizations" that I'd read about lately, so I asked them more about it. What did learning have to do with strategic thinking?

Strategic thinking, they explained, was about using the scientific method, a way of thinking that relies on hypothesis generation and testing. In hypothesizing, you ask the creative "what if" questions. To test your hypothesis, you ask the analytic "if … then … " questions. You adopt a mindset that treats your method of accomplishing your purpose as an experiment. If that experiment fails, you try something else.

Seen this way, strategic thinking is both creative and analytic. It is an iterative process you cycle through continuously, learning something new with each pass that allows you to develop a better hypothesis for the next pass. It is intelligently opportunistic in search of its goals, in a way that enhances the intended strategy, while leaving room for new and unintended strategies to emerge. Test 3, I decided, was definitely a keeper.

Image, intention, flexibility. Really, what more was there to say about strategic thinking? Except maybe, I thought, to ask those orangutans how they got that way. Probably genetic, I thought, or maybe their elders were not only good strategic thinkers themselves, but good teachers of strategic thinking processes as well. At any rate, it was closing time at the zoo, and I couldn't find an exhibit to help me answer that question. Maybe I'll visit the Museum of Science on my next field trip.

Source: *The Journal of Business Strategy* (Emerald Group Publishing Limited), Vol. 18, 1, January/February, 1997: pp. 8–11.

THE MAN VS. THE MACHINE
BY CHARLES KRAUTHAMMER

How better to get into the head of the strategist than putting one against a machine and watching what happens—in the ultimate game of strategy, so it is believed, namely chess. What happens when the machine never makes a mistake, while the man has the ideas? What happens to a man who cannot outcalculate the machine, but can outsmart it? We learn that there is hope for the human after all—for a while at least, says author Charles Krauthammer. Can chess, computers, even strategy, be human after all?

Scoff if you will, but I stayed home Tuesday to watch a chess game. I don't get ESPN in my office, and I was not about to miss the tiebreaking final game of the man versus machine epic: the best humanity has to offer, Garry Kasparov, versus the best in silicon, X3D Fritz.

To most folks, all of this man versus computer stuff is anticlimax. After all, the barrier was broken in 1997 when man was beaten, Kasparov succumbing to Deep Blue in a match that was truly frightening. Frightening not so much because the computer won, but because of how it won, making at some point moves of subtlety. And subtlety makes you think there might be something stirring in all that silicon.

It seems to me obvious that machines will achieve consciousness. After all, we did, and with very humble beginnings.

In biology, neurons started firing millions of years ago, allowing tiny mindless organisms to move about, avoid noxious stimuli, etc. But when enough of those neurons were put together with enough complexity, all of a sudden you got . . . us. A cartoon balloon pops up above that mass of individually unconscious neurons and says, "I exist."

In principle, why should that not eventually occur with silicon? The number of chips and complexity of their interaction will no doubt be staggering and may require centuries to construct. But I do not see why silicon cannot make the same transition from unconsciousness to consciousness that carbon did.

That's the bad news. In the meantime, the good news is that the latest man–machine chess matches are reason for some relief.

Since 1997 machines have gotten so much stronger that even off-the-shelf ones now routinely massacre the ordinary player. But the great players are learning to adapt. Genius is keeping up.

Given Moore's law (computers double in power every 18 months), you would have expected that 6 years after Deep Blue's epic victory, humans would be helpless. In fact, they are not. Earlier this year, Kasparov played a match against Deep Junior and drew. And his four-game match with Fritz, the strongest chess program in the world, ended dead even: two draws and a win each.

Interestingly, in each game that was won, the loser was true to his nature. Kasparov lost Game 2 because, being human, he made a tactical error. Computers do not. When it comes to tactics, they play like God. Make one error, just one, and you're toast. The machine's exploitation of the error will be flawless and fatal.

In Game 3 the computer lost because, being a computer, it has (for now) no imagination. Computers can outplay just about any human when the field is open, the pieces have mobility and there are millions of tactical combinations. Kasparov

The computer lost because, being a computer, it has (for now) no imagination.

therefore steered Game 3 into a position that was utterly static—a line of immobile pawns cutting across the board like the trenches of the First World War.

Neither side could cross into enemy territory. There was, "thought" Fritz, therefore nothing to do. It can see 20 moves deep, but even that staggering foresight yielded absolutely no plan of action. Like a World War I general, Fritz took to pacing up and down behind its lines.

Kasparov, on the other hand, had a deep strategic plan. Quietly and methodically, he used the bit of space he had on one side of the board to align his pieces, preparing for the push of a single pawn down the flank to queen—and win.

Meanwhile, Fritz was reduced to shuffling pieces back and forth. At one point, it moved its bishop one square and then back again on the next move. No human would ever do that. Not just because it is a waste of two moves. It is simply too humiliating. It is an open declaration to your opponent that you have no idea what you're doing, and that maybe checkers is your game.

The observers loved it. "This move showed that the computer doesn't feel any embarrassment," said grandmaster Gregory Kaidanov. It was a moment to savor. Eventually, sons of Fritz will feel embarrassment and much more—why not: We are just cleverly arranged carbon and we feel—but that's still centuries (decades?) away. In the meantime, Kasparov is showing that while we can't outcalculate machines, we can still outsmart them.

It even appears that we—the best of us humans, that is—will be able to hold our own for a while. That's victory enough. For now.

THINK LIKE A GRANDMASTER
BY G. M. ALEXANDER KOTOV

Let us suppose that at one point in your game you have a choice between two moves. R-21 or N-KN5. Which should you play? You settle down comfortably in your chair and start your analysis silently saying to yourself the possible moves. "All right I could play R-21 and he would probably play B-2N2, or he could take my 2RP which is now undefended. What then?" Do I like the look of the position then? You go one move further in your analysis and then you pull a long face—the rook move no longer appeals to you. Then you look at the knight move. "What if I go N-KN5? He can drive it away by P-KR3. I go N-K4, he captures it with his bishop. I recapture and he attacks my queen with his rook. That doesn't look very nice ... so the knight move is no good. Let's look at the rook move again." [more analysis] "No, [that] is no good. I must check the knight move again [more analysis] No good! So, I mustn't move the knight. Try the rook move again ... ." At this point you glance at the clock. "My goodness! Already 30 minutes gone on thinking whether to move the rook or the knight. If it goes on like this you'll really be in time trouble. And then suddenly you are struck by the happy idea—why move rook or knight? What about B-2N1?" And without any more ado, without any analysis at all you move the bishop. Just like that with hardly any consideration at all.

Source: Kotov (1971) *Think Like a Grandmaster*, pp. 15–16, BT Batsford; London.

THE EMPEROR'S NEW SUIT
BY HANS CHRISTIAN ANDERSEN

Somewhere in our brains must be a little place for what is called common sense. So little sometimes that brain researchers have trouble finding it. Sometimes even so little as to disappear entirely. Here comes an old and famous fable about that, about how our egos can strip us of our common sense. As you read it, think of all the corporations you know dressed in their lovely new strategies. And bear in mind the most important lesson of all: That little boy didn't just have the courage to say it; he had the courage to see it. Maybe we have too many adults making strategies.

Once upon a time there lived a vain emperor whose only worry in life was to dress in elegant clothes. He changed clothes almost every hour and loved to show them off to his people.

Word of the emperor's refined habits spread over his kingdom and beyond. Two scoundrels who had heard of the emperor's vanity decided to take advantage of it. They introduced themselves at the gates of the palace with a scheme in mind.

"We are two very good tailors and after many years of research we have invented an extraordinary method to weave a cloth so light and fine that it looks invisible. As a matter of fact it is invisible to anyone who is too stupid and incompetent to appreciate its quality."

The chief of the guards heard the scoundrel's strange story and sent for the court chamberlain. The chamberlain notified the prime minister, who ran to the emperor and disclosed the incredible news. The emperor's curiosity got the better of him and he decided to see the two scoundrels.

"Besides being invisible, your Highness, this cloth will be woven in colors and patterns created especially for you." The emperor gave the two men a bag of gold coins in exchange for their promise to begin working on the fabric immediately.

"Just tell us what you need to get started and we'll give it to you." The two scoundrels asked for a loom, silk, gold thread and then pretended to begin working. The emperor thought he had spent his money quite well: In addition to getting a new extraordinary suit, he would discover which of his subjects were ignorant and incompetent. A few days later, he called the old and wise prime minister, who was considered by everyone as a man with common sense.

"Go and see how the work is proceeding," the emperor told him, "and come back to let me know."

The prime minister was welcomed by the two scoundrels.

"We're almost finished, but we need a lot more gold thread. Here, Excellency! Admire the colors, feel the softness!" The old man bent over the loom and tried to see the fabric that was not there. He felt cold sweat on his forehead.

"I can't see anything," he thought. "If I see nothing, that means I'm stupid! Or, worse, incompetent!"

"What a marvelous fabric," he said then. "I'll certainly tell the emperor." The two scoundrels rubbed their hands gleefully. They had almost made it. More thread was requested to finish the work.

Finally, the emperor received the announcement that the two tailors had come to take all the measurements needed to sew his new suit.

"Come in," the emperor ordered. Even as they bowed, the two scoundrels pretended to be holding a large roll of fabric.

"Here it is your Highness, the result of our labor," the scoundrels said. "We have worked night and day but, at last, the most beautiful fabric in the world is ready for you. Look at the colors and feel how fine it is." Of course the emperor did not see any colors and could not feel any cloth between his fingers. He panicked and felt like fainting. But when he realized that no one could know that he did not see the fabric, he felt better. Nobody could find out he was stupid and incompetent. And the emperor didn't know that everybody else around him thought and did the very same thing.

The farce continued as the two scoundrels had foreseen it. Once they had taken the measurements, the two began cutting the air with scissors while sewing with their needles an invisible cloth.

"Your Highness, you'll have to take off your clothes to try on your new ones." The two scoundrels draped the new clothes on him and then held up a mirror. The emperor was embarrassed but since none of his bystanders were, he felt relieved.

"Yes, this is a beautiful suit and it looks very good on me," the emperor said trying to look comfortable. "You've done a fine job."

"Your Majesty," the prime minister said, "we have a request for you. The people have found out about this extraordinary fabric and they are anxious to see you in your new suit." The emperor was doubtful about showing himself naked to the people, but then he abandoned his fears. After all, no one would know about it except the ignorant and the incompetent.

"All right," he said. "I will grant the people this privilege." He summoned his carriage and the ceremonial parade was formed. A group of dignitaries walked at the very front of the procession and anxiously scrutinized the faces of the people in the street. All the people had gathered in the main square, pushing and shoving to get a better look. An applause welcomed the regal procession. Everyone wanted to know how stupid or incompetent his or her neighbor was but, as the emperor passed, a strange murmur rose from the crowd.

Everyone said, loud enough for the others to hear: "Look at the emperor's new clothes. They're beautiful!"

Look at the emperor's new clothes. They're beautiful!

"What a marvelous train!"

"And the colors! The colors of that beautiful fabric! I have never seen anything like it in my life!" They all tried to conceal their disappointment at not being able to see the clothes, and since nobody was willing to admit his own stupidity and incompetence, they all behaved as the two scoundrels had predicted.

A child, however, who had no important job and could only see things as his eyes showed them to him, went up to the carriage.

"The emperor is naked," he said.

"Fool!" his father reprimanded, running after him. "Don't talk nonsense!" He grabbed his child and took him away. But the boy's remark, which had been heard by the bystanders, was repeated over and over again until everyone cried: "The boy is right! The emperor is naked! It's true!"

The emperor realized that the people were right but could not admit to that. He thought it better to continue the procession under the illusion that anyone who couldn't see his clothes was either stupid or incompetent. And he stood stiffly on his carriage, while behind him a page held his imaginary mantle.

MANAGEMENT EXPERT GARY HAMEL TALKS WITH ENRON'S KEN LAY ABOUT WHAT IT'S LIKE TO LAUNCH A NEW STRATEGY IN THE REAL WORLD
BY GARY HAMEL

This is a byte—or is it a bite?—that helps you get inside the head of management writers: a little glimpse into our cognition. The actual title of the article is "Turning Your Business Upside Down." (About this we offer no comment.) We also wish to note that any resemblance between this fable and the last is purely inside the head of you, the reader. (Look, we all make mistakes. We look forward to what Gary may wish to publish about ours.)

What's America's most innovative company? You probably wouldn't guess Enron, yet it ranked No. 1 in innovation—among 431 companies—in *Fortune's* latest survey of corporate reputations. In the natural gas and electricity industries, CEO Ken Lay is, in Gary Hamel's terms, a revolutionary who has taken his company into new countries, new businesses, and new strategies ....

HAMEL: Ken, what would be the two or three things that you've done that really went against the conventions of the industry? Where has Enron been the rule-breaker?

184 STRATEGY BITES BACK

LAY: Early on, when other natural gas companies were attempting to hold on in a regulated market, we were pushing hard to move our business upstream into unregulated businesses. We thought there'd be more opportunity here to differentiate ourselves on products and services and make a profit at it. Many other companies felt they needed to stay in the regulated pipeline business just to survive. You see a little of the same mentality today in the electrical industry.

      More profoundly, we believed there were abundant supplies of natural gas worldwide, and shortages in the 1970s were just caused by regulation. So we were trying to substitute natural gas for all other fuels, particularly for coal and nuclear as electricity generators—and this was when the U.S. and Europe had legal prohibitions against building new natural gas power plants. Despite all that, our idea was that natural gas was, in fact, an ideal fuel for power generation—probably the best both economically and environmentally. And that has led to a total paradigm shift in the power business worldwide.

HAMEL: You brought a lot of new skills and people in to Enron. You now have, for example, Wall Street traders who help you exploit arbitrage opportunities in energy markets and who help customers manage financial risks. One of my arguments has always been that revolutions often get created by people from outside an industry.

LAY: Right. Historically it was thought that natural gas was natural gas was natural gas. But you also have a lot of risk management or contract issues. Do customers want to buy short-term or long-term? Do they want to hedge their risk? Or do they want to go with the market index? Now everybody can have the kind of portfolio they want, the kind of risk they want to take, and the kind of exposure they want to price swings.

HAMEL: So you've decommoditized the ultimate commodity.

LAY: To some extent we have. And in the process, of course, you acquire the kind of skills you need. We not only had to attract talent from investment banking houses, commercial banks, and elsewhere, but also had to compete against them. We also had to go up against the big consulting firms for some of the new MBAs coming out of our graduate schools.

HAMEL: So you really did bring a lot of new voices into Enron, who had different perspectives, different kinds of industry experience?

LAY: Very much so. And that's got to help shake the whole culture. In some ways, when you go through a profound restructuring, long years of experience in your industry really turn out to be a detriment, not an asset . . . .

HAMEL: Ken, are there things you're doing at Enron to institutionalize the generation of new ideas and new strategies?

LAY: I'm not saying this can happen in every type of business, but we're breaking up our profit centers into smaller pieces. As you move down the organization—what August is talking about—you can have some really bright, capable people who are not able to spread their wings, not able to try the things they want to try. In a smaller operation they can, and of course we found that, in most cases, whenever we do this, it accelerates growth. Probably the most obvious place we've done that recently is our Enron Capital

& Trade Resources, which provides all these risk-management, long-term contract, financing, and other type services to the gas and electricity industries in the U.S. and abroad. It was being run as one unit and is now being run effectively as five units, and I expect we'll break it even further.

HAMEL: But I guess one of the thoughts is that certainly there is no assumption that strategy and innovation start only at the top.

LAY: No, absolutely not. It's a matter of making sure you get more people down in those operations and that they have a more active role. Doing that really lets them determine the strategy for their unit, where maybe in a bigger unit they wouldn't have much impact ... I think the one lesson probably all CEOs need to learn—at least I certainly needed to learn—is, you have to be very reluctant to tell somebody they shouldn't do something. Quite often someone will come up with an idea, and I have to keep myself from saying, "We just don't want to go in that direction." By doing that, I've learned that a lot of things that initially looked to me to be unreachable, undoable, or maybe even unwise, turned out to be brilliant after a lot of work. And I think if you start shutting down some of those ideas early, well then, of course, your employees won't come to you at all.

Source: Reprinted in excerpted form from "Turning Your Business Upside Down: management expert Gary Hamel talks with Enron's Ken Lay about what it's like to launch a new strategy in the real world." *Fortune*, Gary Hamel © 1997, Time Inc. All rights reserved.

CHAPTER 7

STRATEGY A STEP AT A TIME

"We are much more likely to act our way into a new way of thinking than to think our way into a new way of acting."
(Karl Weick)

"The pencil is mightier than the pen."
(Pirsig, in Lila)

"It is very dangerous to try to leap a chasm in two bounds."
(Chinese proverb)

"Ready—Fire—Aim."
(Cadbury executive, quoted in Peters and Waterman, In Search of Excellence, 1982)

– *Planning: Ready—aim—aim*

– *Entrepreneurship: Fire—fire—fire*

– *Learning: Ready—fire—aim—fire—aim— ....*

INTRODUCTION TO CHAPTER 7

From cognition to behavior. And from the head to the organization. Now we get a very different view of strategy. It emerges, one step at a time, as all kinds of people solve all kinds of problems and exploit all kinds of opportunities, all of which converge into the patterns we call strategies.

      This means that everyone can be a strategist, just so long as he or she gets out of the back office—away from the calculating, the pondering, the figuring—and *does* things to find out what should be figured, pondered, and calculated. The process is called strategic *learning*.

      When strategy seems like mission impossible, with so many complicated things to be taken into account, in a world that seems so chaotic, what to do? The answer: something. Take a single step, somewhere. Let yourself at least learn. You won't develop the strategy all at once, like Moses being handed the tablets at the top of the mountain, but it might emerge, step by step, as people adapt together over time.

      In keeping with this view, many of our bytes in this chapter are bits: little pieces of the puzzle of how organizations learn their strategies: cartoons, poems, comments of all kinds (lots of them colorful). We won't go through them here all piece by piece, only to say that you will find everything from a description of muddling with a purpose and "talk the walk" to stories about Honda and Intel for real, and little bits about strategists as bees and flies, strategies that grow in hothouses and up like weeds, plus some sensible advice from Gary Hamel about how to grow strategies. And finally a couple of little bites—about the dangers of doing things a step at a time.

GOOD MANAGERS DON'T MAKE POLICY DECISIONS
BY H. EDWARD WRAPP

That we are in the realm of something very different is demonstrated by this first byte, even its title: "Good Managers Don't Make Policy Decisions." Here, we find out what strategy taken one step at a time really means. Don't be fooled by the masculine gender in this article, or the use of the word *policy* instead of *strategy*, which were common when the article was published in 1967—this is a fully contemporary article, in a way a lot more so than many of the fancy, formalized techniques hyped these days. "Finding the corridors of comparative indifference," "avoiding policy straitjackets," and "muddling with a purpose" never go out of date!

The upper reaches of management are a land of mystery and intrigue. Very few people have ever been there, and the present inhabitants frequently send back messages that are incoherent both to other levels of management and to the world in general. This may account for the myths, illusions, and caricatures that permeate the literature of management—for example, such widely held notions as these:

> Life gets less complicated as a manager reaches the top of the pyramid.

> The manager at the top level knows everything that's going on in the organization, can command whatever resources he may need, and therefore can be more decisive.
> The general manager's day is taken up with making broad policy decisions and formulating precise objectives.
> The top executive's primary activity is conceptualizing long-range plans.
> In a large company, the top executive may be seen meditating about the role of his organization in society.

I suggest that none of these versions alone, or in combination, is an accurate portrayal of what a general manager does ... What common characteristics, then, do successful executives exhibit *in reality*? I shall identify five skills or talents which, in my experience, seem especially significant ....

Keeping well informed

First, each of my heroes has a special talent for keeping himself informed about a wide range of operating decisions being made at different levels in the company. As he moves up the ladder, he develops a network of information sources in many different departments. He cultivates these sources and keeps them open no matter how high he climbs in the organization. When the need arises, he bypasses the lines on the organization chart to seek more than one version of a situation ....

Top-level managers are frequently criticized by writers, consultants, and lower levels of management for continuing to enmesh themselves in operating problems after promotion to the top rather than withdrawing to the "big picture." Without any doubt, some managers do get lost in a welter of detail and insist on making too many decisions. Superficially, the good manager may seem to make the same mistake—but his purposes are different. He knows that only by keeping well informed about the decisions being made can he avoid the sterility so often found in those who isolate themselves from operations. If he follows the advice to free himself from operations, he may soon find himself subsisting on a diet of abstractions, leaving the choice of what he eats in the hands of his subordinates . . . .

Focusing time and energy
The second skill of the good manager is that he knows how to save his energy and hours for those few particular issues, decisions, or problems to which he should give his personal attention. He knows the fine and subtle distinction between keeping fully informed about operating decisions and allowing the organization to force him into participating in these decisions or, even worse, making them. Recognizing that he can bring his special talents to bear on only a limited number of matters, he chooses those issues which he believes will have the greatest long-term impact on the company, and on which his special abilities can be most productive. Under ordinary circumstances he will limit himself to three or four major objectives during any single period of sustained activity.

What about the situations he elects not to become involved in as a decision maker? He makes sure (using the first skill mentioned) that the organization keeps him informed about them at various stages; he does not want to be accused of indifference to such issues. He trains his subordinates not to bring the matters to him for a decision . . . . When he sees a problem where the organization needs his help, he finds a way to transmit his know-how short of giving orders—usually by asking perceptive questions.

Playing the power game

To what extent do successful top executives push their ideas and proposals through the organization? The rather common notion that the "prime mover" continually creates and forces through new programs, like a powerful majority leader in ... Congress, is in my opinion very misleading.

The successful manager is sensitive to the power structure in the organization. In considering any major current proposal, he can plot the position of the various individuals and units in the organization on a scale ranging from complete, outspoken support down to determined, sometimes bitter, and oftentimes well-cloaked opposition. In the middle of the scale is an area of comparative indifference. Usually, several aspects of a proposal will fall into this area, and *here is where he knows he can operate*. He assesses the depth and nature of the blocs in the organization. His perception permits him to move through what I call *corridors* of comparative indifference. He seldom challenges when a corridor is blocked, preferring to pause until it has opened up.

Related to this particular skill is his ability to recognize the need for a few trial-balloon launchers in the organization. He knows that the organization will tolerate only a certain number of proposals which emanate from the apex of the pyramid. No matter how sorely he may be tempted to stimulate the organization with a flow of his own ideas, he knows he must work through idea men in different parts of the organization. As he studies the reactions of key individuals and groups to the trial balloons these men send up, he is able to make a better assessment of how to limit the emasculation of the various proposals. For seldom does he find a proposal which is supported by all quarters of the organization. The emergence of strong support in certain quarters is almost sure to evoke strong opposition in others.

Value of sense of timing

Circumstances like these mean that a good sense of timing is a priceless asset for a top executive … As a good manager stands at a point in time, he can identify a set of goals he is interested in, albeit the outline of them may be pretty hazy. His timetable, which is also pretty hazy, suggests that some must be accomplished sooner than others, and that some may be safely postponed for several months or years. He has a still hazier notion of how he can reach these goals. He assesses key individuals and groups. He knows that each has its own set of goals, some of which he understands rather thoroughly and others about which he can only speculate. He knows also that these individuals and groups represent blocks to certain programs or projects, and that these points of opposition must be taken into account. As the day-to-day operating decisions are made, and as proposals are responded to both by individuals and by groups, he perceives more clearly where the corridors of comparative indifference are. He takes action accordingly.

The art of imprecision

The fourth skill of the successful manager is knowing how to satisfy the organization that it has a sense of direction *without ever actually getting himself committed publicly to a specific set of objectives.* This is not to say that he does not have objectives—personal and corporate, long-term and short-term. They are significant guides to his thinking, and he modifies them continually as he better understands the resources he is working with, the competition, and the changing market demands. But as the organization clamors for statements of objectives, these are samples of what they get back from him:

> *"Our company aims to be number one in its industry."*
> *"Management's goal is to meet its responsibilities to stockholders, employees, and the public."*

Maintaining viability

In my opinion, statements such as these provide almost no guidance to the various levels of management. Yet they are quite readily accepted as objectives by large numbers of intelligent people. Why does the good manager shy away from precise statements of his objectives for the organization? The main reason is that he finds it impossible to set down specific objectives which will be relevant for any reasonable period into the future. Conditions in business change continually and rapidly, and corporate strategy must be revised to take the changes into account. The more explicit the statement of strategy, the more difficult it becomes to persuade the organization to turn to different goals when needs and conditions shift.

The public and the stockholders, to be sure, must perceive the organization as having a well-defined set of objectives and a clear sense of direction. But in reality the good top manager is seldom so certain of the direction which should be taken. Better than anyone else, he senses the many, many threats to his company—threats which lie in the economy, in the actions of competitors, and, not least, within his own organization.

He also knows that it is impossible to state objectives clearly enough so that everyone in the organization understands what they mean. Objectives get communicated only over time by a consistency or pattern in operating decisions. Such decisions are more meaningful than words. In instances where precise objectives are spelled out, the organization tends to interpret them so they fit its own needs.

Subordinates who keep pressing for more precise objectives are in truth working against their own best interests. Each time the objectives are stated more specifically, a subordinate's range of possibilities for operating are reduced. The narrower field means less room to roam and to accommodate the flow of ideas coming up from his part of the organization.

Avoiding policy straitjackets

The successful manager's reluctance to be precise extends into the area of policy decisions. He seldom makes a forthright statement of policy. He may be aware that in some companies there are executives who spend more time in arbitrating disputes caused by stated policies than in moving the company forward. The management textbooks contend that well-defined policies are the sine qua non of a well-managed company. My research does not bear out this contention . . . .

Since able managers do not make policy decisions, does this mean that well-managed companies operate without policies? Certainly not. But the policies are those which evolve over time from an indescribable mix of operating decisions. From any single operating decision might have come a very minor dimension of the policy as the organization understands it; from a series of decisions comes a pattern of guidelines for various levels of the organization.

The skillful manager resists the urge to write a company creed or to compile a policy manual. Preoccupation with detailed statements of corporate objectives and departmental goals, and with comprehensive organization charts and job descriptions—this is often the first symptom of an organization which is in the early stages of atrophy . . . .

A detailed spelling out of objectives may only complicate the task of reaching them. Specific, detailed statements give the opposition an opportunity to organize its defenses.

Muddling with a purpose

The fifth, and most important, skill I shall describe bears little relation to the doctrine that management is (or should be) a comprehensive, systematic, logical, well-programmed science. Of all the heresies set forth here, this should strike doctrinaires as the rankest of all!

The successful manager, in my observation, recognizes the futility of trying to push total packages or programs through the organization. He is willing to take less than total acceptance in order to achieve modest progress toward his goals. Avoiding debates on principles, he tries to piece together particles that may appear to be incidentals into a program that moves at least part of the way toward his objectives. His attitude is based on optimism and persistence. Over and over he says to himself, "There must be some parts of this proposal on which we can capitalize."

Whenever he identifies relationships among the different proposals before him, he knows that they present opportunities for combination and restructuring. It follows that he is a man of wide-ranging interests and curiosity. The more things he knows about, the more opportunities he will have to discover parts which are related. This process does not require great intellectual brilliance or unusual creativity. The wider ranging his interests, the more likely that he will be able to tie together several unrelated proposals. He is skilled as an analyst, but even more talented as a conceptualizer.

If the manager has built or inherited a solid organization, it will be difficult for him to come up with an idea which no one in the company has ever thought of before. His most significant contribution may be that he can see relationships which no one else has seen . . . .

Many of the articles about successful executives picture them as great thinkers who sit at their desks drafting master blueprints for their companies. The successful top executives I have seen at work do not operate this way. Rather than produce a full-grown decision tree, they start with a twig, help it grow, and ease themselves out on the limbs only after they have tested to see how much weight the limbs can stand ....

Rather than produce a full-grown decision tree, they start with a twig, help it grow, and ease themselves out on the limbs only after they have tested to see how much weight the limbs can stand.

[The effective manager, then, spots] *opportunities and relationships in the stream of operating problems and decisions.* [But]—lest it be concluded from the description of this skill that the good manager is more an improviser than a planner, let me emphasize that he is a planner and encourages planning by his subordinates. Interestingly, though, professional planners may be irritated by a good general manager. Most of them complain about his lack of vision. They devise a master plan, but the president (or other operating executive) seems to ignore it, or to give it minimum acknowledgment by borrowing bits and pieces for implementation. He ... knows that even if the plan is sound and imaginative, the job has only begun. The long, painful task of implementation will depend on his skill, not that of the planner.

Source: Reprinted by permission of *Harvard Business Review* from "Good Managers Don't Make Policy Decisions" by H. Edward Wrapp, September/October 1967. Copyright © by The Harvard Business School Publishing Corporation; all rights reserved.

BACKING INTO A BRILLIANT STRATEGY: REPORTS ON HONDA

In 1959, Honda, a Japanese manufacturer of motorcycles, not (yet) automobiles, entered the American market. By 1966, it had 63 percent of that market. Partly the company beat American and British manufacturers in selling large motorcycles to what was the initial market: macho, black-leather: jacket types. And partly it created a new market for small motorcycles driven by ordinary people, thanks to a legendary advertising campaign called "You meet the nicest people on a Honda." The company had in fact been producing these small motorcycles for the Japanese market since the 1940s, when Takeo Fujisawa convinced his partner, Sochiro Honda, whose love was designing and racing big motorcycles, that many of the Japanese people could not afford automobiles post-war but would be amenable to small inexpensive motorcycles for regular transportation.

The British government, whose motorcycle manufacturers saw their share of the import market drop from 49 to 10 percent in that 1959–1966 period, hired the Boston Consulting Group to explain what happened and suggest how their manufacturers could come back. BCG replied, in 1975, in a report that became famous, and formed the basis for cases written at schools such as Harvard and UCLA.

Two excerpts from that report are reproduced here, to give the sense of it. This is followed by the transcript of parts of an interview held by Richard Pascale, co-author of *The Art of Japanese Management* (1981), who had his doubts about the BCG report, with the Honda managers who were responsible for the entry into the American market. The story speaks for itself; so does the contrast between the two interpretations.

Various excerpts related to these two stories are then reproduced.

From the Boston consulting group report

The success of the Japanese motorcycle industry originated with the growth of their domestic market during the 1950s. [By 1960] ... they had developed huge production volumes in small motorcycles in their domestic market, and volume-related cost reductions had followed. This resulted in a highly competitive cost position which the Japanese used as a springboard for penetration of world markets with small motorcycles in the early 1960s ....

The Japanese motorcycle industry, and in particular Honda, the market leader, present a [consistent] picture. The basic philosophy of the Japanese manufacturer is that high volumes per model provide the potential for high productivity as a result of using capital-intensive and highly automated techniques. Their marketing strategies are therefore directed toward developing these high-volume models, hence the careful attention that we have observed them giving to growth and market share, and then in production, the cost reduction potential is realized in practice as a result of a primary focus on production engineering and investment for cost reduction.

Source: *Strategy Alternatives for the British Industry*, Boston Consulting Group, 1975.

From the interview with the Honda managers
In truth we had no strategy other than the idea of seeing if we could sell something in the United States ... [We had] to obtain a currency allocation from the Ministry of Finance. They were extraordinarily skeptical. Toyota had launched the Toyopet in the U.S. in 1958 and had failed miserably. "How could Honda succeed?" they asked. Months went by. We put the project on hold. Suddenly, five months after our application, we were given the go-ahead—but at only a fraction of our expected level of commitment. "You can invest $250,000 in the U.S. market," they said, "but only $110,000 in cash." The remainder of our assets had to be in parts and motorcycle inventory ....

In truth we had no strategy other than the idea of seeing if we could sell something in the United States.

Our focus ... was to compete with the European exports. We knew our products at the time were good but not far superior. Mr. Honda was especially confident of the 250cc and 305cc machines. The shape of the handlebar on these larger machines looked like the eyebrow of Bhudda, which he felt was a strong selling point. Thus, after some discussion and with no compelling criteria for selection, we configured our start-up inventory with 25 percent of each of our four products—the 50cc Supercub, and the 125cc, 250cc, and 305cc. In dollar-value terms, of course, the inventory was heavily weighted toward the larger bikes.

The stringent monetary controls of the Japanese government together with the unfriendly reception we had received during our 1958 visit caused us to start small. We chose Los Angeles, where there was a large second- and third-generation Japanese community, a climate suitable for motorcycle use, and a growing population. We were so strapped for cash that the three of us shared a furnished apartment that we rented for $80 per month. Two of us slept on the floor. We obtained a warehouse in a run-down section of the city and waited for the ship to arrive. Not daring to spare our funds for equipment, the three of us stacked the motorcycle crates three high—by hand—swept the floors, and built and maintained the parts bin.

We were entirely in the dark the first year. We were not aware that the motorcycle business in the United States occurs during a seasonal April-to-August window—and our timing coincided with the closing of the 1959 season. Our hard-learned experiences with distributorships in Japan convinced us to try to go to the retailers direct. We ran ads in the motorcycle trade magazine for dealers. A few responded. By spring of 1960, we had 40 dealers and some of our inventory in their stores—mostly larger bikes. A few of the 250cc and 305cc bikes began to sell. Then disaster struck. By the first week of April 1960, reports were coming in that our machines were leaking oil and encountering clutch failure. This was our lowest moment. Honda's fragile reputation was being destroyed before it could be established. As it turned out, motorcycles in the United States are driven much farther and much faster than in Japan. But not knowing that, we had to dig deeply into our precious cash reserves to air freight our motorcycles to the Honda testing lab in Japan. Throughout the dark month of April, Pan Am was the only enterprise in the U.S. that was nice to us. Our testing lab worked 24 hour days bench testing the bikes to try to replicate the failure. Within a month, a redesigned head gasket and clutch spring solved the problem. But in the meantime, events had taken a surprising turn.

Throughout our first eight months, following Mr. Honda's and our own instincts, we had not attempted to move the 50cc Supercubs. While they were a smash success in Japan (and manufacturing couldn't keep up with demand there), they seemed wholly unsuitable for the U.S. market where everything was bigger and more luxurious. As a clincher, we had our sights on the import market—and the Europeans, like the American manufacturers, emphasized the larger machines.

We used the Honda 50s ourselves to ride around Los Angeles on errands. They attracted a lot of attention. One day we had a call from a Sears buyer. While persisting in our refusal to sell through an intermediary, we took note of Sears's interest. But we still hesitated to push the 50cc bikes out of fear they might harm our image in a heavily macho market. But when the larger bikes started breaking, we had no choice. We let the 50cc bikes move.

Source: From an article originally entitled "Perspectives on Strategy: The Real Story Behind Honda's Success." Copyright © 1996 by the Regents of the University of California. Reprinted from the *California Management Review*, Vol. 27, No. 1. By permission of the Regents.

COMPARE SOME OF THE WORDS USED IN THE BCG REPORT ON HONDA WITH SOME OF THE WORDS USED BY THE HONDA MANAGERS

BCG words

> Highly competitive cost position
> Used as a springboard
> Penetration
> Consistent picture
> Careful attention ... to growth and market share

Honda managers' words

> No strategy
> Selling something
> In the dark the first year
> Events had taken a surprising turn
> We had no choice

UNITED STATES IMPORTS OF MOTORCYCLES AND PARTS

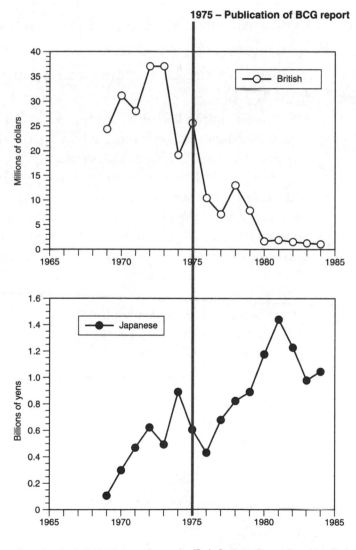

Source: *Strategy Alternatives for the British Industry*, Commodity Trade Statistics, Boston Consulting Group, 1975.

WHATEVER HAPPENED TO THE BRITISH MOTORCYCLE INDUSTRY?

Bert Hopwood was an executive of BSA, one of the major British motorcycle producers at the time Honda was entering the U.S. market. Here are excerpts from his book:

> "Not a soul on the Parent Board [meaning full-time senior executives in the corporate headquarters] knew the first thing about single track vehicles."

> "... in the early 1960s [at precisely the time when the Honda managers were in Los Angeles riding their motorcycles] ... the chief executive of a world-famous group of management consultants tried hard to convince me that it is ideal that top-level management executives should have as little knowledge as possible relative to the product. This great man really believed that this qualification enabled them to deal effectively with all business matters in a detached and uninhibited way ...."

Source: *Whatever Happened to the British Motorcycle Industry?* by Bert Hopwood, San Leandro, CA: Haynes Publishing, 1981.

RUMINATIONS ON HONDA
BY RICHARD RUMELT

Richard Rumelt used to use the BCG Honda case in his strategy course at UCLA.

In 1977, my MBA exam on the Honda Motorcycle case asked "Should Honda enter the global automobile business?" It was a "giveaway" question. Anyone who said "yes" flunked.

> Markets were saturated.
> Efficient competitors existed in Japan, the United States, and Europe.
> Honda had little or no experience in automobiles.
> Honda had no auto distribution system.

In 1985, my wife drove a Honda.

"If you know how to design a great motorcycle engine, I can teach you all you need to know about strategy in a few days. If you have a Ph.D. in strategy, years of labor are unlikely to give you ability to design great new motorcycle engines."

Source: *Many Faces of Honda* by Richard Rumelt, 1995: pp. 9–10.

BEES AND FLIES MAKING STRATEGY
BY GORDON SIU

"If you place in a bottle half a dozen bees and the same number of flies, and lay the bottle horizontally, with its base [the closed end] to the window, you will find that the bees will persist, till they die of exhaustion or hunger, in their endeavor to discover an [opening] through the glass; while the flies, in less than two minutes, will all have sallied forth through the open neck on the opposite side . . . .

It is [the bees] love of flight, it is their very intelligence, that is their undoing in this experiment. They evidently imagine that the issue from every prison must be where the light shines clearest; and they act in accordance, and persist in too-logical action. [To bees] glass is a supernatural mystery . . . and, the greater their intelligence, the more inadmissible, more incomprehensible, will the strange obstacle appear. Whereas the feather-brained flies, careless of logic . . . flutter wildly hither and thither, and meeting the good fortune that often waits on the simple . . . necessarily end up by discovering the friendly opening that restores their liberty to them."

Source: Quote by Gordon Siu from *In Search of Excellence* by T. H. Peters and R. H. Waterman, New York: Harper and Row, 1982: p. 108.

Henry, Bruce and Joe's Moral of the Story: We need more flies making strategy and fewer bees.

GROWING STRATEGIES: TWO WAYS
BY HENRY MINTZBERG

So, at the extremes, we have two views of the strategy process. In this byte, one of us compares them by using metaphors from the earth.

The Hothouse model (for bees)

1. *There is only one strategist, and that person is the chief executive officer. (Other managers may participate; planners provide support.)*
2. *The CEO formulates strategies through a conscious, controlled process of thought, much as tomatoes are cultivated in a hothouse.*
3. *These strategies come out of this process fully developed, then to be made formally explicit, much as ripe tomatoes are picked and sent to the market.*
4. *These explicit strategies are then formally implemented (which includes the development of the necessary budgets and programs as well as the design of the appropriate structure).*
5. *To manage this process is to analyze the appropriate data, preconceive insightful strategies, and then plant them carefully, caring for them and watching them as they grow on schedule.*

The Grassroots model (for flies)

1. *Strategies grow initially like weeds in a garden, they are not cultivated like tomatoes in a hothouse.* In other words, the process of strategy formation can be overmanaged; sometimes it is more important to let patterns emerge than to force an artificial consistency upon an organization prematurely. The hothouse, if needed, can come later.

2.   *These strategies can take root in all kinds of places, virtually anywhere people have the capacity to learn and the resources to support that capacity.* Sometimes an individual or unit in touch with a particular opportunity creates his, her, or its own pattern. This may happen inadvertently, when an initial action sets a precedent. At other times, a variety of actions converge on a strategic theme through the mutual adjustment of various people, whether gradually or spontaneously. The external environment can also impose a pattern on an unsuspecting organization. The point is that organizations cannot always plan where their strategies will emerge, let alone plan the strategies themselves.

3.   *Such strategies become organizational when they become collective—that is, when the patterns proliferate to pervade the behavior of the organization at large.* Weeds can proliferate and encompass a whole garden; then the conventional plants may look out of place. Likewise, emergent strategies can sometimes displace the existing deliberate ones. But, of course, what is a weed but a plant that wasn't expected? With a change of perspective, the emergent strategy, like the weed, can become what is valued (just as Europeans enjoy salads of the leaves of America's most notorious weed, the dandelion!).

4.   *The processes by which the initial patterns work their way through the organization need not be consciously intended, by formal leaders or even informal ones.* Patterns may simply spread by collective action, much as plants proliferate. Of course, once strategies are recognized as valuable, the processes by which they proliferate can be managed, just as plants can be selectively propagated.

5.   *New strategies, which may be emerging continuously, tend to pervade the organization during periods of change, which punctuate periods of more integrated continuity.* Put more simply, organizations, like gardens, may accept the biblical maxim of a

time to sow and a time to reap (even though they can sometimes reap what they did not mean to sow). Periods of convergence, during which the organization exploits its prevalent, established strategies, tend to be interrupted by periods of divergence, during which the organization experiments with and subsequently accepts new strategic themes . . . .

6   *To manage this process is not to preconceive strategies but to recognize their emergence and intervene when appropriate.*

A destructive weed, once noticed, is best uprooted immediately. But one that seems capable of bearing fruit is worth watching, indeed sometimes even worth building a hothouse around. To manage in this context is to create the climate within which a wide variety of strategies can grow . . . and then to watch what does in fact come up. But [management] must not be too quick to cut off the unexpected . . . Moreover, management must know when to resist change for the sake of internal efficiency and when to promote it for the sake of external adaptation. In other words, it must sense when to exploit an established crop of strategies and when to encourage new strains to displace them . . . .

Source: *Mintzberg on Management: Inside our Strange World of Organizations* by Henry Mintzberg, New York: Free Press, 1989: pp. 214–216.

STRATEGIES THAT LEARN
BY GARY HAMEL

Here is Gary Hamel at his best—an insightful piece that brings the open view of strategy to life, with sensible advice:

The dirty little secret of the strategy industry is that it doesn't have any theory of strategy creation. Whenever we come across a brilliantly successful strategy, we are all inclined to ask, "Was it luck, or was it foresight? Did these guys have this thing all figured out, or did they just stumble into success?"

The dirty little secret of the strategy industry is that it doesn't have any theory of strategy creation.

A key thing to remember is that truly innovative strategies are always, and I mean always, the result of lucky foresight. Foresight, however, doesn't emerge in a sterile vacuum; it emerges in the fertile loam of experience, coincident trends, unexpected conversations, random musings, career detours, and unfulfilled aspirations. But the question remains. Can we do anything to increase the fertility of the soil out of which strategy grows? Can we make serendipity happen? Or at least encourage it? I think so.

One good place to start is to develop a deep theory of strategy creation. It's clear that strategizing isn't a "thing," and neither is it a process. Instead, it must be a deeply embedded capability—a way of understanding what's really going on in your industry, turning it on its head, and then envisioning the new opportunities that fall out.

Strategizing is not a once-a-year rain dance, nor is it a once-a-decade consulting project. Strategizing must be a skill as deeply embedded as total quality, cycle-time reduction, or customer service. Just as business processes can be reinvented in ways big and small, so too can business models. This is how new wealth gets created.

Here are five ways organizations can radically rethink their missions.

New voices

Companies miss the future not because they are fat or lazy but because they are blind. That blindness is a genetic blindness. Land is a mystery to fish—fish are not genetically equipped to understand land. And by the time fish learn about land it is often too late. Many companies are genetically unequipped to see where the future is coming from. A lack of genetic diversity makes it difficult for companies to first encompass and then exploit the various trends and discontinuities that could be leveraged to create new wealth. New voices (i.e., new genetic material) must be brought into the strategy process. Diversity was a requirement for the development of life; so too is it a requirement for the emergence of new strategy ....

New conversations

Strategy depends not only on a diversity of voices but on the connections between those voices as well. For strategy to emerge, we need new conversations—conversations that cross the boundaries of function, technology, hierarchy, business, and geography. One thing is certain: if for 5 or 6 years in a row the same 10 or 15 people in a company have the same conversations about strategy in the same way, new insights will be unlikely to emerge. Strategizing depends on creating a rich and complex web of conversations that cut across previously isolated pockets of knowledge and create new and unexpected combinations of insight . . . .

Conversations cannot be hurried. Conversations cannot be tightly scripted. They certainly cannot be shoehorned into the typical planning process or a two day strategy "retreat" at a posh hotel.

We often lament the fact that it takes so long for a new strategy to rise through the layers of a bureaucratic organization to the level of management where resources can be allocated. At one time or another, many companies have set up orphanages for such ideas—typically labeled "new venture divisions." But imagine a strategy process where you put senior management (the people who hold all the resources) directly alongside the folks who have typically been disenfranchised from the strategy process—young people stationed out in the field and newcomers . . . .

New perspectives
One can't raise an individual's IQ, but it is possible to help someone see the world in new ways. If you ever took an economics course, you probably didn't enjoy it at first. But one day something clicked, and you began to see the world through a new lens. Suddenly you understood how interest rates get determined, how supply and demand work to set prices, and what things influence exchange rates. You became enlightened. Great strategy requires new ways of seeing. Redefining what a company does best constitutes a new way of seeing . . . .

But it is not only a new lens that can provide enlightenment; so too can a new vantage point. Sometimes a company simply cannot see the future from where it is standing. For example, Nokia, a Finnish company that makes cellular phones and is based at the edge of the Arctic, may be ill-positioned to track lifestyle trends on the other side of the planet—trends that could ultimately redefine its industry. One possible solution—send Finnish engineers to Venice Beach in California, down Kings Road in London, or to other places on the planet where new lifestyle trends get set. Immerse those engineers in the new cultural milieu; change their experience base ... Opportunities for innovative strategy don't emerge from sterile analysis and number crunching—they emerge from novel experiences that can create opportunities for novel insights. As the songwriter Jimmy Buffet succinctly put it, "Changes in latitudes, changes in attitudes."

New passions
We've too often ignored the emotional side of strategy. If strategy is partly about collective purpose and a sense of shared destiny, don't we need to recognize this explicitly in the way we go about creating strategy? For example, has anyone out there looked explicitly at the issue of commitment? I don't mean the commitment of financial resources by senior executives, but the emotional commitment of individuals at the bottom of the organization who are being asked to devote their lives to carrying out a new strategy ....

I believe that one way of raising commitment is to get individuals throughout the organization deeply involved in the process of creating strategy. Individuals, I would argue, should have a say in determining the destiny of the organizations to which they devote their efforts ....

I believe that inside almost every individual is a deep passion for discovery and novelty. We try new restaurants, take vacations in new places, and search out new experiences of all kinds. I always find it amazing to see the passions that are unleashed when an organization goes to its members and invites them to participate in charting their collective destiny ....

Experimentation

Passion and foresight will only get you so far. When it comes to executing a strategy, the end target may be clearly visible—"I want to climb that mountain over there"—but much of the route may be invisible from the starting point. The only way you're going to see the path ahead is to start moving. Thus strategy is as much about experimentation as it is about foresight and passion.

In many organizations, the quest for efficiency drives out experimentation. One question I often ask managers: "Can you point to 20 or 30 small experiments going on in your company that you believe could fundamentally remake your company?" In most cases, the answer is no, there is nothing to point to ....

The breadth of experimentation must be related to the degree of unknowability that confronts the firm ... Kent Foster, president of GTE, puts the problem of unknowability this way: "We are talking about products that are still evolving, delivered to a market that is still emerging, via a technology that is still changing on a daily basis." This must sound familiar to any executive trying to chart a course through the chaotic frenzy that is the new economy. Clearly, experimentation is a must in this environment ....

The more experimentation, the faster a company can understand precisely which strategies are likely to work. The goal is not to develop "perfect" strategies, but to develop strategies that take us in the right direction, and then progressively refine them through rapid experimentation and adjustment ....

Source: Original title: "Killer Strategies That Make Shareholders Rich," *Fortune*, Gary Hamel, 1997, Time Inc. All rights reserved.

The more experimentation, the faster a company can understand precisely which strategies are likely to work.

STRATEGY UP AND DOWN
BY JOHN KOTTER AND MICHAEL BEER ET AL.

John Kotter and Michael Beer taught at the Harvard Business School; their offices were steps apart. They each published an article in the *Harvard Business Review* on steps to effective change, eight in one, six in the other. But that is where the similarity ends. One encourages top-down change, the other bottom-up.

If the experts can't agree, what are the practitioners to do?

Top-down transformation by John Kotter

1.   *Establishing a sense of urgency*: Examining market and competitive realities; identifying and discussing crises, potential crises, or major opportunities

2.   *Forming a powerful guiding coalition*: Assembling a group with enough power to lead the change effort; encouraging the group to work together as a team

3.   *Creating a vision*: Creating a vision to help direct the change effort; developing strategies for achieving that vision

4.   *Communicating the vision*: Using every vehicle possible to communicate the new vision and strategies; teaching new behaviors by the example of the guiding coalition

5.   *Empowering others to act on the vision*: Getting rid of obstacles to change; changing systems or structures that seriously undermine the vision; encouraging risk-taking and non-traditional ideas, activities, and actions

6.   *Planning for and creating short-term wins*: Planning for visible performance improvements; creating those improvements; recognizing and rewarding employees involved in the improvements

7.   *Consolidating improvements and producing still more changes*: Using increased credibility to change systems, structures, and policies that don't fit the vision; hiring, promoting, and developing employees who can implement the vision; reinvigorating the process with new projects, themes, and change agents

8.   *Institutionalizing new approaches*: Articulating the connections between the new behaviors and corporation success; developing the means to ensure leadership development and succession

Bottom-up change by Michael Beer, Russell Eisenstat, and Bert Spector

1. *Mobilize commitment to change through joint diagnosis of business problems*: By helping people develop a shared diagnosis of what is wrong in an organization and what can and must be improved, a general manager [of a unit] mobilizes the initial commitment that is necessary to begin the change process.

2. *Develop a shared vision of how to organize and manage for competitiveness*: Once a core group of people is committed to a particular analysis of the problem, the general manager can lead employees toward a task-aligned vision of the organization that defines new roles and responsibilities.

3. *Foster consensus for the new vision, competence to enact it, and cohesion to move it along.*

4. *Spread revitalization to all departments without pushing it from the top*: The temptation to force newfound insights on the rest of the organization can be great, particularly when rapid change is needed, but it would be the same mistake that senior managers make when they try to push programmatic change throughout a company. It short-circuits the change process. It's better to let each department "reinvent the wheel"—that is, to find its own way to the new organization.

5. *Institutionalize revitalization through formal policies, systems, and structures:* The new approach has to become entrenched.

6 *Monitor and adjust strategies in response to problems in the revitalization process*: The purpose of change is to create ... a learning organization capable of adapting to a changing competitive environment: Some might say that this is the general manager's responsibility. But monitoring the change process needs to be shared.

STRATEGY IS DESTINY
A REVIEW OF THE ROBERT BURGELMAN BOOK BY HARVEY SCHACHTER

What are the practitioners to do when the experts can't agree on top-down and bottom-up? Both, says this byte. That's what Intel did and it seemed to work. This byte comes from a review of the book by Robert Burgelman, *Strategy Is Destiny*, by Canadian business journalist Harvey Schachter.

Intel Corp. is famed for its Pentium computer chip and its dominance in the microprocessor market. Yet its move into that area of business was resisted by senior management and not a result of deliberate planning.

Senior management failed to appreciate the significance of a key decision by mighty International Business Machines Corp. to use Intel's 8088 microprocessor in its first personal computer in 1981. Indeed, when developing the microprocessor, management hadn't even included PCs on the list of 50 possible applications for the hardware.

A group of innovative lower-level managers and engineers who were close to customers led the strategic shift that saved Intel's bacon, as the market for semiconductor memory— which had been the company's initial focus and was still higher management's prime concern—wilted.

Robert Burgelman, a professor of management at Stanford University, relates that story in *Strategy Is Destiny*, a book based on more than a decade of unusual access to the company's senior management, and a stint co-teaching a course on strategic management with Intel's former chief executive officer, Andy Grove.

Mr. Burgelman outlines two main forms of strategic planning, top-down and bottom-up (or "induced" and "autonomous," to use the academic jargon of the book). Most companies use both, consciously or unconsciously. But the mix between them can be crucial. Intel essentially used top-down in its first epoch, from 1968 to 1985, under founder Gordon Moore, but its open culture allowed for the bottom-up initiative that saved the day. In the second epoch, from 1985 to 1998, Mr. Grove was much more controlling and top-down strategic management helped the company to prosper, although it also meant several potentially promising ventures were choked off, not given the financial or moral support that might have made Intel stronger today.

"I weed out the weeds but also some of the potential seeds," he admitted.

He failed to see the value of Intel chipsets—integrated circuits that later were combined with the Pentium into a powerful package.

Fortunately, as the lower-level manager who oversaw the effort said, "We didn't let the chief executive officer of the company tell us something we believed in couldn't happen." Mr. Grove, to his credit, sent a concessionary note after he was proved wrong: "And I said it couldn't be done."

But the chipset fared better than other products not blessed by management because at least it was closely tied to the

We didn't let the chief executive officer of the company tell us something we believed in couldn't happen.

main focus at the company. Other products that would have taken the company along a different course weren't so lucky. And the company was slow to shift into networking, even losing the executive championing that effort.

Mr. Burgelman calls that strategic inertia—when a company is so focused on its strategy that it is slow to embrace other alternatives. Possibilities that are complementary to the main strategy get twisted to fit it, even if that isn't necessarily the best way to develop the new initiative. Ventures that don't fit with the core strategy need to pay as they go if they are to survive—and many don't.

In the third epoch, which began under current CEO Craig Barrett, Intel is consciously trying to blend top-down and bottom-up strategy. There are many factors that have to be balanced to make this work, including the way the company internally chooses between competing initiatives and the way outside interests make the same choices.

Mr. Burgelman argues that to be successful, management must deliberately strike a balance between top-down and bottom-up strategy throughout a company's evolution . . . .

Source: Originally published in the *Globe and Mail*, Toronto, Ontario, Canada, Monday, June 17, 2002: Section C1.

TALK THE WALK
BY KARL WEICK

Karl Weick has a charming way of turning around conventional wisdom. Here, in "Talk the Walk," he shows how we have to act in order to think—that is, do in order to learn, to make sense of the world, implement, if you like, in order to formulate. This byte allows us to make sense of what we have been reading in this chapter.

Managers are repeatedly urged to practice what they preach so others will take their preaching seriously and try to implement it in their own work. Hypocrisy is the culprit here and to exorcise it, managers are told to "walk the talk" . . . .
        [P]art of the reason people fail when they try to walk the talk is that their intention was doomed from the start. Failure was inevitable because they have things backward. Walking is the means to find things worth talking about. People discover what they think by looking at what they say, how they feel, and where they walk. The talk makes sense of walking, which means those best able to walk the talk are the ones who actually talk the walking they find themselves doing most often, with most intensity, and with most satisfaction. How can I know what I value until I see where I walk? People make sense of their actions, their walking, their talking. If they are forced to walk the talk, this may heighten accountability, but it also is likely to heighten caution and inertia and reduce risk taking and innovation. This outcome occurs not just because people are scared. It occurs

because people who are forced to walk the talk prematurely often forgo exploration and walk on behalf of words that they barely understand. Because things that are poorly understood are things that tend to be seen as uncontrollable, they seem like threats rather than opportunities. Innovation shuts down.

People act in order to think, as, for example, when they talk in order to see what they think. Or, in the language [here], people walk in order to find what is worth talking about . . . .

Source: Karl Weick, *Sensemaking in Organizations*, 182–183, copyright 1995 by Sage Publications. Reprinted by permission of Sage Publications.

People act in order to think, as, for example, when they talk in order to see what they think.

HOW TO FIGHT THE STRATEGIC WARS
NAPOLEON AND THE DUKE OF WELLINGTON

"If I appeared to be ever ready and equal on any occasion, it is because I thought over matters for long before I undertake to do the slightest thing; I have foreseen all eventualities." (Napoleon)

"I know not what I do, for everything depends on events. I have not a will of my own but expect everything from their outcome." (Napoleon)

"He calculated the little things in advance with great precision; whereas his worldwide designs were originated, transformed, improvised, in accordance with circumstances and developments."
(Napoleon's biographer)

"They planned their campaigns just as you might make a splendid piece of harness. It looks very well, and answers very well until it gets broken; and then you are done for. Now I made my campaigns of ropes. If anything went wrong, I tied a knot and went on." (Duke of Wellington)

LOOKING A FEW STEPS BACK

Two little stories to end this chapter; one prose, one poetry. They really say the same thing: Beware of incrementalism, of one little stop at a time that can take us down the garden path. Maybe these two bite-sized steps will drive the message home better than one.

The U.S. standard railroad gauge (distance between the rails) is 4 feet 8.5 inches. That is an exceedingly odd number. Why was that gauge used? Because that's the way they built them in England, and the U.S. railroads were built by English expatriates. Why did the English build them that way? Because the first rail lines were built by the same people who built the pre-railroad tramways, and that's the gauge they used. Why did "they" use that gauge? Because the people who built the tramways used the same jigs and tools that they used for building wagons, which used that wheel spacing.

So why did the wagons have that particular odd spacing? Well, if they tried to use any other spacing, the wagon wheels would break on some of the old, long-distance roads in England, because that was the spacing of the wheel ruts.

So who built those old rutted roads? The first long-distance roads in Europe (and England) were built by Imperial Rome for their legions. The roads have been used ever since. And the ruts in the roads? The ruts in the roads, which everyone had to match for fear of destroying their wagon wheels, were first formed by Roman war chariots. Since the chariots were made for (or by) Imperial Rome, they were all alike in the matter of wheel spacing.

The U.S. standard railroad gauge of 4 feet 8.5 inches derives from the original specification for an Imperial Roman war chariot. Specifications and bureaucracies live forever. So the next time you are handed a specification and wonder what horse's ass came up with it, you may be exactly right, because the Imperial Roman war chariots were made just wide enough to accommodate the back end of two war horses. Thus we have the answer to the original question.

Now for the twist to the story. When we see a space shuttle sitting on its launching pad, there are two booster rockets attached to the side of the main fuel tank. These are solid rocket boosters, or SRBs. The SRBs are made by Thiokol at their factory in Utah. The engineers who designed the SRBs might have preferred to make them a bit fatter, but the SRBs had to be shipped by train from the factory to the launch site. The railroad from the factory had to run through a tunnel in the mountains. The tunnel is slightly wider than the railroad track, and the railroad track is about as wide as two horses' rumps. So, a major design feature of what is arguably the world's most advanced transportation system was determined over two thousand years ago by the width of a horse's ass!

Don't you just love engineering?

THE CALF PATH
SAM WALTER FOSS (1895)

One day thru the primeval wood
A calf walked home, as good calves should,
But made a trail, all bent askew,
A crooked trail, as all calves do.

Since then 300 years have fled,
And I infer the calf is dead,
But still, he left behind his trail
And thereby hangs my moral tale.

The trail was taken up next day
By a lone dog, that passed that way.
And then a wise bell weathered sheep
Pursued the trail, o'er vale and steep
And drew the flocks behind him too
As good bell weathered always do.
And from that day o'er hill and glade
Thru those old woods, a path was made.

And many men wound in and out,
And dodged, and turned, and bent about,
And uttered words of righteous wrath
Because 'twas such a crooked path.
But still they followed, do not laugh
The first migrations of that calf.
And thru the winding woods they stalked
Because he wobbled when he walked.

The forest path became a lane
That bent, and turned, and turned again.
This crooked lane became a road
Where many a poor horse with his load
Toiled on beneath the burning sun
And traveled some three miles in one.
And thus a century and a half
They trod the footsteps of that calf.

The years passed on in swiftness fleet,
The road became a village street;
And thus, before we were aware,
A city's crowded thoroughfare.
And soon the central street was this
Of a renowned metropolis;
And men two centuries and a half
Trod in the footsteps of that calf.

Each day a hundred thousand rout
Followed this zigzag calf about
And o'er his crooked journey went
The traffic of a continent.

A hundred thousand men were led
By one calf near three centuries dead.
They followed still his crooked way,
And lost one hundred years a day;
For thus such reverence is lent
To well-established precedent.

A moral lesson this might teach,
Were I ordained and called to preach;
For men are prone to go it blind,
Along the calf-paths of the mind;
And work away from son to son,
To do what other men have done,
They follow in the beaten-track,
An out and in, and forth and back,
And still their devious course pursue,
To keep the path that others do.
They keep the path a sacred groove,
Along which all their lives they move.
But how the wise old wood gods laugh,
Who saw the first primeval calf!
Ah! Many things this tale might teach.
But I am not ordained to preach.

STRATEGY WITH THE GLOVES OFF AND THE HALO ON

"He who excuses himself accuses himself."
(Molière)

"The trouble with being in a rat race is that even if you win, you are still a rat."
(Lily Tomlin)

"Quality has two enemies: quantity and equality."
(Salvador de Madariaga)

"Not everything is unsayable in words, only the living truth."
(Ionesco)

INTRODUCTION TO CHAPTER 8

By now you can appreciate that there is more to strategy than SWOT, planning, and spreadsheets. In fact there is more to it than thinking and seeing and learning too. Strategy has two other dimensions that should never be forgotten (not that one ever lets you, even if the other tries to make you): the yang of politics, namely pulling apart, and the yin of culture, or pulling together—one with the gloves off, the other with the halo on. These are opposite forces in a sense, and some of the bytes of this chapter will make that clear. But a couple of others will show just how fine a line there can be between them, and how they can sometimes work in concert.

Politics has two aspects, micro and macro, if you like. One is manifested by political games within the organization, as different interest groups try to pull it apart for their own benefit. Strategy (among other things) can be a fierce battleground over scarce resources and future direction. The other is when the whole organization acts politically, protecting or advancing its own needs and so pulling apart from the society at large, sometimes using nasty ploys, other times creating cozy coalitions.

Culture is quite different. Here people rally around the organization and pull together. That can obviously be beneficial; strategy is significantly about cooperation. Think of culture like a hand-crafted Persian rug: beautiful and difficult to create, so, perhaps the first line of defense for competitive advantage. Culture is about deep-rooted traditions and unique ways of doing things, woven together around values and beliefs.

But this indicates its weakness too. A strong culture weaves everything so tightly that it becomes difficult to change anything. How do you replace a strand or two that has worn out in a nice old Persian rug? And does that rug allow you to focus elsewhere? In other words, culture encourages people to see only what they want to see, which is usually consistent with what has long been seen. So culture helps to maintain stability, while it discourages change, strategic and otherwise.

We begin with a couple of short colorful descriptions, about how chess pieces and bees fight among themselves. Then we have a byte on how to play political games in organizations, followed by a bite on planning as public relations—namely how this ostensible tool of rational analysis can reduce to covert politics.

Next we listen to a famous consultant about how companies can use "brinkmanship" for competitive (or is it cooperative?) advantage. Seduction comes next: We are, after all, considering politics here, except that in this byte it begins to look a little like culture. In the next reading, we find that culture can look a lot like strategy.

And then it's on to a couple of final bites; one on how to kill a culture—changing it may be difficult, killing it is easy—the other on how to build a bad culture—not so hard either. Ask the monkeys.

CHESS IN THE REAL WORLD
BY FELIX HOLT

Fancy what a game of chess would be if all the chessmen had passions and intellects, more or less small and cunning; if you were not only uncertain about your adversary's men, but a little uncertain also about your own; if your Knight could shuffle himself on to a new square on the sly; if your Bishop, in disgust at your Castling, could wheedle your Pawns out of their places; and if your Pawns, hating you because they are Pawns, could make away from their appointed posts that you might get checkmate on a sudden. You might be the longest headed of deductive reasoners, and yet you might be beaten by your own Pawns. You would be especially likely to be beaten, if you depended arrogantly on your mathematical imagination, and regarded your passionate pieces with contempt.

George Eliot (1980) *Felix Holt, The Radical*, Oxford: Clarendon Press, p. 237.

BEES IN THE REAL WORLD
BY EDWARD O. WILSON

In the first case, two groups of messengers (bees) had got into competition; one group announced a nesting place to the northwest, the other to the northeast. Neither of the two wished to yield. The swarm finally flew off and I could scarcely believe my eyes—it sought to divide itself. The one half wanted to fly to the northwest, the other to the northeast. Apparently each group of scouting bees wanted to abduct the swarm to the nesting place of its choice. But that was not naturally possible, for one group was always without the queen, and there resulted in a remarkable tug of war in the air once 100 meters to the northwest, then again 150 meters to the northeast, until finally after half an hour the swarm gathered at the old location. Immediately both groups began with their soliciting dances, and it was not until the next day that the northeast group finally yielded; they ended their dances and thus an agreement was reached on the nesting place in the northwest.

LAWS OF POWER
BY ROBERT GREENE AND JOOST ELFFERS

Robert Greene and Joost Elffers published a best-selling book titled *The 48 Laws of Power*. These are derived from a review of the great political philosophers, conmen, and notorious figures of all time. We select here some of those which have the greatest relevance for strategy. Note that some of these laws contradict—like the eighth one and the last one. That suggests that if you are going to play political games, you are going to have to do some careful thinking. As in every other aspect of strategy.

Conceal your intentions

Keep people off balance and in the dark by never revealing the purpose behind your actions. Without a clue about what you are up to, they cannot prepare a defense. Guide them far enough down the wrong path, envelop them in enough smoke, and by the time they realize your intentions it will be too late.

Win through your actions, never through argument

Any momentary triumph you think you have gained through argument is really a Pyrrhic victory; the resentment and ill will you stir up is stronger and lasts longer than any momentary change of opinion. It is much more powerful to get others to agree with you through your actions, without saying a word. Demonstrate; do not explicate.

Crush your enemy totally

All great leaders since Moses have known that a feared enemy must be crushed completely. (Sometimes they have learned this the hard way.) If one ember is left alight, no matter how dimly it smolders, a fire will eventually break out. More is lost through stopping halfway than through total annihilation; the enemy will recover, and will seek revenge. Crush him, not only in body but also in spirit.

Keep others in suspense—cultivate an air of unpredictability

Humans are creatures of habit with an insatiable need to see familiarity in other people's actions. Your predictability gives them a sense of control. Turn the tables; be deliberately unpredictable. Behavior that seems to have no consistency or purpose will keep them off balance, and they will wear themselves out trying to explain your moves. Taken to an extreme, this strategy can intimidate and terrorize.

Use the surrender tactic

Transform weakness into power when you are weaker, never fight for honor's sake; choose surrender instead. Surrender gives you time to recover, time to torment and irritate your conqueror, time to wait for his power to wane. Do not give him the satisfaction of fighting and defeating you. By turning the other cheek you infuriate and unsettle him. Make surrender a tool of power.

Concentrate your forces

Conserve your forces and energies by concentrating them at their strongest point. You gain more by finding a rich mine and mining it deeper than by flitting from one shallow mine to another, intensity defeats extensity every time . . . .

Re-create yourself

Do not accept the roles that society foists on you. Re-create yourself by forging a new identity, one that commands attention and never bores the audience. Be the master of your own image rather than letting others define it for you. Incorporate dramatic devices into your public gestures and actions. Your power will be enhanced and your character will seem larger than life.

Plan all the way to the end

The ending is everything. Plan all the way to it, taking into account all the possible consequences, obstacles, and twists of fortune that might reverse your hard work and give the glory to others. By planning to the end you will not be overwhelmed by circumstances and you will know when to stop. Gently guide fortune and help determine the future by thinking far ahead.

Control the options—get others to play with the cards you deal

The best deceptions are the ones that seem to give the other person a choice; your victims feel they are in control, but are actually your puppets. Give people options that come out in your favor whichever one they choose. Force them to make choices between the lesser of two evils, both of which serve your purpose. Put them on the horns of a dilemma; they will be gored wherever they turn.

Master the art of timing

Never seem to be in a hurry; hurrying betrays a lack of control over yourself, and over time. Always seem patient, as if you know that everything will come to you eventually. Become a detective of the right moment; sniff out the spirit of the times, the trends that will carry you to power. Learn to stand back when the time is not yet ripe, and to strike fiercely when it has reached fruition.

Stir up waters to catch fish
Anger and emotion are strategically counterproductive. You must always stay calm and objective. But if you can make your enemies angry while staying calm yourself, you gain a decided advantage. Throw your enemies off balance; find the chink in their vanity through which you can rattle them and you hold the strings.

Disarm and infuriate with the mirror effect
The mirror reflects reality, but it is also the perfect tool for deception; when you mirror your enemies, doing exactly as they do, they cannot figure out your strategy. The mirror effect mocks and humiliates them, making them overreact. By holding up a mirror to their psyches, you seduce them with the illusion that you share their values; by holding up a mirror to their actions, you teach them a lesson. Few can resist the power of the mirror effect.

Preach the need for change, but never reform too much at once
Everyone understands the need for change in the abstract, but on the day-to-day level people are creatures of habit. Too much innovation is traumatic and will lead to revolt. If you are new to a position of power, or an outsider trying to build a power base, make a show of respecting the old way of doing things. If change is necessary, make it feel like a gentle improvement on the past.

Do not go past the mark you aimed for; in victory, learn when to stop
The moment of victory is often the moment of greatest peril. In the heat of victory, arrogance and overconfidence can push you past the goal you aimed for, and by going too far you make more enemies than you defeat. Do not allow success to go to your head. There is no substitute for strategy and careful planning. Set a goal, and when you reach it, stop.

Assume formlessness

By taking a shape, by having a visible plan, you open yourself to attack. Instead of taking a form for your enemy to grasp, keep yourself adaptable and on the move. Accept the fact that nothing is certain and no law is fixed. The best way to protect yourself is to be as fluid and formless as water; never bet on stability or lasting order. Everything changes.

Source: From *The 48 Laws of Powers* by Robert Greene and Joost Elffers, © 1998 by Robert Greene and Joost Elffers. Used by permission of Viking Penguin, a division of Penguin Group (USA) Inc.

PLANNING AS PUBLIC RELATIONS
BY HENRY MINTZBERG

Everything in organizational life can get politicized—even that ultimately rational tool of systematic analysis, namely planning. This bite describes how planning gets used, in government and business, for promotion, or public relations, and how that becomes political.

Some organizations use planning as a tool, not because anyone necessarily believes in the value of the process per se but because influential outsiders do. Planning thus becomes a game. It's called "public relations."

　　　　This view of planning as a facade to impress outsiders is supported by no shortage of evidence. As an example of what he called planning as a "gesture process" to suggest the "trappings of objectivity," Nutt (1984) cited those "city governments [that] hire consultants to do 'strategic planning' to impress bond rating agencies," and "firms [that] posture with each other and the marketplace with their claims of long-range planning." In universities, Cohen and March (1976) described plans that "become symbols": for example, "an organization that is failing can announce a plan to succeed," one that lacks a piece of equipment can announce a plan to get it. They also discussed plans that "become advertisements," noting that "what is frequently called a 'plan' by a university is really an investment brochure," one "characterized by pictures, by *ex cathedra* pronouncements of excellence, and by the absence of most relevant information."

Langley (1988) found this to be true of the public sector in general, where public relations was "probably a very common motivation for 'strategic planning,'" although "the same kind of role is played by subsidiaries and/or autonomous divisions who have to produce 'strategic plans' for their parent firms."

Wildavsky (1973) has pointed out that national leaders who "wish to be thought modern ... have a document with which to dazzle their visitors," one that "no one who matters attends to." In fact, it "need not be a means of surmounting the nation's difficulties, but rather may become a mode of covering them up." And why shouldn't they do this? After all, "capitalist America insisted upon a plan" in return for its foreign aid to poor countries: "It did not matter whether the plan worked; what did count was the ability to produce a document which looked like a plan."

Presumably to be able to plan is tantamount to being able to spend money responsibly. To quote Lorange and Vancil (1977):

> *Announcing that his organization would undertake a formal program of strategic planning was almost like a public announcement that he was going to quit smoking. It forced the chief executive to attempt to change his own behavior in a way that he knew was desirable.*

But did he?

In a narrow sense, of course, some planning for the purposes of public relations seems to be justified. After all, supermarkets need their capital, the developing nations their aid, universities their support. In the poorer nations, national planning "may be justified on a strictly cash basis: Planners may bring in more money from abroad than it costs to support them at home" (Wildavsky, 1973).

But in a broader sense, is this kind of planning justified at all? Leaving aside the obvious waste of resources on a collective basis—the money that could be saved if everyone stopped playing the game—public relations planning probably distorts priorities in the organization itself. In poor nations, for example, it misallocates skills that are in very short supply, capabilities that could be devoted to solving real problems (or doing useful planning!). Even in more developed countries, think of how much time and talent has been wasted over the years. Worse, what is intended as public relations can be taken seriously when it should not be.

Organizations that are forced to articulate strategies that are not really there—because their managements lack the necessary vision, or because they are still engaged in a complex learning process in order to create their strategies—get caught up in all kinds of wasteful behaviors. One is the pronouncement of platitudes—ostensible strategies that no one has any intention of implementing, even if that were possible.

Reading Colonel Summers's (1981) account of the articulation of U.S. military strategy since World War II, one gets the impression of pronouncements racing like mad to keep up with the emerging reality. For example, after the Korean War, the Field Service Regulations acknowledged "wars of limited objective" and removed "victory" as a necessary aim of war; by 1962, cold war was acknowledged!

Some of the more dysfunctional side effects of public relations planning are suggested in Benveniste's (1972) discussion of what he called "trivial planning."

1.   There is a tendency to use past trends to predict future developments (i.e., predict "more of the same") . . . the experts are not asking any difficult questions. They take the status quo for granted. They raise no policy options . . . .

2.   Trivial planning exercises are well-publicized ... Everyone is encouraged to participate and have his or her say. The plan is published and widely distributed. The document is beautifully printed, and the less content it has, the longer it becomes.

3.   Trivial planning is sequential ... No sooner has one set of experts made its bland recommendations than another set is studying the same problem or some appropriate variant ... Most trivial planning is undertaken by ephemeral bodies: task forces, presidential commissions, and the like. These bodies have the dual advantage of relying on prestigious outsiders, thus adding to the body's visibility, and providing these experts with insufficient time to find out how they might effect changes ....

4.   Trivial planning tends to be used by conservatives ... Since the planning movements espouse a mild reformist ideology, and since planning is perceived as an attempt to bring about change, providing technocratic legitimacy is more useful to policies that preserve a conservative stance.

In his book on the French national planning experience, Cohen (1977) concluded that "planning is either political or it is decorative." But decorative (i.e., public relations) planning can easily become political, pitting outsiders in search of control against insiders seeking protection. The same can happen internally when planning becomes a device to impress the senior management, which Cohen and March (1976) referred to as "an administrative test of will":

> *If a department wants a new program badly enough, it will spend a substantial amount of effort in "justifying" the expenditure by fitting it into a "plan." If an administrator wishes to avoid saying "yes" to everything, but has no basis for saying "no" to anything, he tests the commitment of the department by asking for a plan.*

Add all this together, and public relations planning becomes a device by which almost everyone, no matter how obsessed with gaining control, loses it. Outsiders get useless pronouncements, and junior managers waste time filling out forms while senior managers get distracted from the more important issues. Only the planners come out on top in some perverse way, not for how they benefit the organization so much as themselves. And that makes such planning for them fundamentally political.

Thus, in the final analysis, much as in the experiences of the Communist states, planning that is used artificially, for image instead of substance, does not help managers or outside influencers to control organizations or even the environments of those organizations. Nor does it enable planners to do so. Rather, that inanimate system called planning ties everyone in knots and so ends up controlling everybody!

Source: *The Rise and Fall of Strategic Planning*, by Henry Mintzberg, New York: Free Press, 1994. Excerpt with deletions from pp. 214–219.

References
Benveniste, A. (1972) *The Politics of Expertise*, Berkeley, CA: Glendessary Press, pp. 105–118.

Cohen, S. S. (1977) *Modern Capitalist Planning: The French Model*, Berkeley, CA: University of California Press, p. xv.

Cohen, M. D. and March, J. G. (1976) "Decisions, Presidents and Status" in March, J. G. and Olsen, J. P., Eds, *Ambiguity and Choice in Organizations*, Bergen, Norway: Universitetsforlaget, p. 195.

Langley, A. (1988) "The Roles of Formal Strategic Planning," *Long Range Planning*, 21, 3, 1988, pp. 40–50.

Lorange, P. and Vancil, R. F. (1977) *Strategic Planning Systems*, Englewood Cliffs, NJ: Prentice Hall, p. 16.

Nutt, P. C. (1984) "A Strategic Planning Network for Non-Profit Organizations," *Strategic Management Journal*, 5, 1, January/March, 1984, pp. 57–75.

Summers, H. G. Jr. (1981) *On Strategy: The Vietnam War in Context*, Strategic Studies Institute, US Army College.

Wildavsky, A. (1973) "If Planning Is Everything Maybe It's Nothing," *Policy Sciences*, 4, 1973, pp. 127–153.

BRINKMANSHIP IN BUSINESS
BY BRUCE HENDERSON

Once again, we have yin and yang. We start with yang: BCG founder Bruce Henderson's views on brinkmanship in business—cooperating to compete, reaching agreements with opponents. Very interesting advice for any big strategist in a big strategic game. If you are female and put off by the use of the masculine idiom—businessmen, he, his etc.—bear in mind not only that this was first published in 1979, but also that this is about brinkmanship—a rather male and indeed macho view of strategy—yang if you like. Yin comes next.

Unfortunately, some businessmen and students perceive competition as some kind of impersonal, objective, colorless affair, with a company competing against the field as a golfer competes in medal play. A better case can be made that business competition is a major battle in which there are many contenders, each of whom must be dealt with individually. Victory, if achieved, is more often won in the mind of a competitor than in the economic arena.

I shall emphasize two points. The first is that the management of a company must persuade each competitor voluntarily to stop short of a maximum effort to acquire customers and profits. The second point is that persuasion depends on emotional and intuitive factors rather than on analysis or deduction.

The negotiator's skill lies in being as arbitrary as necessary to obtain the best possible compromise without actually destroying the basis for voluntary mutual cooperation of self-restraint. There are some commonsense rules for success in such an endeavor:

1. Be sure that your rival is fully aware of what he can gain if he cooperates and what it will cost him if he does not.

2. Avoid any action which will arouse your competitor's emotions, since it is essential that he behave in a logical, reasonable fashion.

3. Convince your opponent that you are emotionally dedicated to your position and are completely convinced that it is reasonable . . . .

Friendly competitors

It may strike most businessmen as strange to talk about cooperation with competitors. But it is hard to visualize a situation in which it would be worthwhile to pursue competition to the utter destruction of a competitor. In every case there is a greater advantage to reducing the competition on the condition that the competitor does likewise. Such mutual restraint is cooperation, whether recognized as such or not . . . .

Businessmen should notice the similarity between economic competition and the peace-time behavior of nations. The object in both cases is to achieve a voluntary, cooperative restraint on the part of otherwise aggressive competitors. Complete elimination of competition is almost inconceivable. The goal of the hottest economic war is an agreement for coexistence, not annihilation. The competition and mutual encroachment do not stop; they go on forever. But they do so under some measure of mutual restraint.

Cold war tactics

A breakdown in negotiations is inevitable if both parties persist in arbitrary positions which are incompatible. Yet there are major areas in business where some degree of arbitrary behavior is essential for protecting a company's self-interest. In effect, a type of brinkmanship is necessary. The term was coined to describe cold war international diplomacy, but it describes a normal pattern in business too.

In a confrontation between parties who are in part competitors and in part cooperators, deciding what is attainable requires an evaluation of the other party's degree of intransigence. The purpose is to convince him that you are arbitrary and emotionally committed while trying to discover what he would really accept in settlement. The competitor known to be coldly logical is at a great disadvantage. Logically, he can afford to compromise until there is no advantage left in cooperation. If, instead, he is emotional, irrational, and arbitrary, he has a great advantage.

Consequence

The heart of business strategy for a company is to promote attitudes on the part of its competitors that will cause them either to restrain themselves or to act in a fashion which management deems advantageous. In diplomacy and military strategy the key to success is very much the same.

The most easily recognized way of enforcing cooperation is to exhibit obvious willingness to use irresistible or overwhelming force. This requires little strategic skill, but there is the problem of convincing the competing organization that the force will be used without actually resorting to it (which would be expensive and inconvenient) . . . .

The nonlogical strategy
The goal of strategy in business, diplomacy, and war is to produce
a stable relationship favorable to you with the consent of your
competitors. By definition, restraint by a competitor is
cooperation. Such cooperation from a competitor must seem to be
profitable to him. *Any competition which does not eventually
eliminate a competitor requires his cooperation to stabilize the situation.*
The agreement is usually that of tacit nonaggression; the
alternative is death for all but one competitor. A stable
competitive situation requires an agreement between competing
parties to maintain self-restraint. Such agreement cannot be
arrived at by logic. It must be achieved by an emotional balance of
forces. This is why it is necessary to appear irrational to
competitors. For the same reason, you must seem unreasonable
and arbitrary in negotiations with customers and suppliers.

      Competition and cooperation go hand in hand in all
real-life situations. Otherwise, conflict could only end in
extermination of the competitor. There is a point in all situations
of conflict where both parties gain more or lose less from peace
than they can hope to gain from any foreseeable victory. Beyond
that point cooperation is more profitable than conflict. But how
will the benefits be shared?

      In negotiated conflict situations, the participant who is
coldly logical is at a great disadvantage. Logically, he can afford to
compromise until there is no advantage left in cooperation. The
negotiator/competitor whose behavior is irrational or arbitrary has
a great advantage if he can depend upon his opponent being
logical and unemotional. The arbitrary or irrational competitor
can demand far more than a reasonable share and yet his logical
opponent can still gain by compromise rather than breaking off
the cooperation . . . .

      Utter destruction of a competitor is almost never
profitable unless the competitor is unwilling to accept peace.

In our daily social contracts, in our international affairs, and in our business affairs, we have far more ability to damage those around us than we ever dare use. Others have the same power to damage us. The implied agreement to restrain our potential aggression is all that stands between us and eventual elimination of one by the other. Both war and diplomacy are mechanisms for establishing or maintaining this self-imposed restraint on all competitors. The conflict continues, but within the implied area of cooperative agreement.

    ... the art of diplomacy can be described as the ability to be unreasonable without arousing resentment. It is worth remembering that the objective of diplomacy is to include cooperation on terms that are relatively more favorable to you than to your protagonist without actual force being used.

    More business victories are won in the minds of competitors than in the laboratory, the factory, or the marketplace. The competitor's conviction that you are emotional, dogmatic, or otherwise nonlogical in your business strategy can be a great asset. This conviction on his part can result in an acceptance of your actions without retaliation, which would otherwise be unthinkable. More important, the anticipation of nonlogical or unrestrained reactions on your part can inhibit his competitive aggression.

Rules for the strategist
If I were asked to distill the conditions and forces described into advice for the business-strategist, I would suggest five rules:
1.   You must know as accurately as possible just what your competition has at stake in his contact with you. It is not what you gain or lose, but what he gains or loses that sets the limit on his ability to compromise with you.

2.   The less the competition knows about your stakes, the less advantage he has. Without a reference point, he does not even know whether you are being unreasonable.

3.   It is absolutely essential to know the character, attitudes, motives, and habitual behavior of a competitor if you wish to have a negotiating advantage.

4.   The more arbitrary your demands are, the better your relative competitive position—provided you do not arouse an emotional reaction.

5.   The less arbitrary you seem, the more arbitrary you can in fact be.

These rules make up the art of business brinkmanship. They are guidelines for winning a strategic victory in the minds of competitors. Once this victory has been won, it can be converted into a competitive victory in terms of sales volume, costs, and profits.

Source: "Brinkmanship in Business" by Bruce Henderson in *Henderson on Corporate Strategy*, Cambridge, MA: Abt books, 1979: pp. 27–33.

STRATEGY AND THE ART OF SEDUCTION
BY JEANNE LIEDTKA

Now yin. Another side to the power issue, much more subtle, from Jeanne Liedtka, the master of the metaphor: how strategy is the art of seduction. If you want to get others to accept your strategy, seduce them (so to speak). Strategy has come a long way baby!

The real power of strategy lies in its ability to seduce. If leaders paid as much attention to *seduction* as to *deduction* in their strategy-making processes, their organizations would be much improved. To put it bluntly: If you want to achieve strategic success, use strategy to treat employees like lovers instead of prostitutes.

If you want to achieve strategic success, use strategy to treat employees like lovers instead of prostitutes.

I spend a lot of time with managers desperately seeking some way to re-energize a workforce deadened by downsizing resources and escalating demands. That conversation often feels as if I've wandered into a national political convention—all gloss and teeth, family values, and fake diversity. But when you peel back the empty words and get to the core, it's still business as usual. And business as usual—command and control—is not working as well as it used to. The reasons behind this are many, and have been discussed endlessly elsewhere. I believe that it comes down ultimately to getting people to care, to change, to adopt new behaviors. If a strategy-making process doesn't make it easier to get people to change, it's useless. Why talk about strategy if everything is OK the way it is?

None of this is new news to anyone. Everything that we know about how human beings change tells us that people don't do it just because we ask them to. And yet strategy, in most of the organizations that I work with, is almost always about "telling." This idea that strategy (unlike wisdom) can be "told" is based on a number of fallacious assumptions that leaders make. Primary among these is that leaders see the strategies that they invent as "real" and "true." But because they see these strategies as "real" and "true" rather than as products of their own invention, they believe that if they merely (and, of course, one should not underestimate the difficulty of even this) communicate it clearly, others will also see it as real and true, and work to implement it. But this assumption cannot be supported.

No strategy is ever "true"—all strategies are inventions. They are man-made designs. Business is not governed by natural laws—our strategies are not "discovered" truths, like $e=mc^2$. Business leaders make them up because they want the future to be different than the past. This is good, and such inventions play a useful purpose—something else that we also know from change theory. But because leaders are so close to their own inventions, and because these inventions flow out of the way they see the world, leaders believe that their strategies are as compelling to others as they are to them. After all, leaders normally have analysis to "prove" that their inventions are true. But you can never "prove" that an invented design for a possible future is "true"—especially using a rationale that flows out of a single view of "reality."

Let me return to my original premise—consider the dating/mating corollary to this approach. I spy the man of my dreams across a crowded room. Seeking him out, I take pains to communicate very clearly that I have thought a lot about our future and wish to inform him what it looks like so that he can work with me to make it happen. I patiently list the reasons why it makes so much sense—after all, I explain, I have really thought this out—and have the spreadsheets to prove it. Maybe I even remember to tell him what his role is and to emphasize that he will be well-compensated for his efforts. Suppose I notice that he does not seem to be paying the kind of close attention that I expect, so I patiently repeat my message—then find it incomprehensible when he nods politely and excuses himself to find the bar.

Successful strategies are compelling and persuasive in the eye of the beholder—put more vividly, they are *seductive*. The real power of any strategy is the opportunity it affords to entice people into sharing an image of the future. Notice that I said *entice*—not delude or manipulate. This is not an easy task for a leader to pull off. After all, success in most industries today requires being willing to make a commitment to something new and different, probably a bit murky and risky—to step away from the security of what has worked in the past and into the uncertainty of the future. It is not an easy sell, in even the most skilled hands. It's a lot like venturing into a new relationship. So what can business leaders learn from the timeless art of seduction?

First, it starts with a *conversation*, not an edict. It works best if the other party goes willingly, when you issue an invitation instead of a command. And it's a contact sport—you get engaged when you're part of the action, not watching from the sidelines. (In fact, the whole process looks pretty humorous to the cynics on the sidelines—it's easy to make fun of their struggles when you've got no skin in the game.)

Second, not just any conversation will do—we need a conversation that starts with a focus on the *possibilities*, rather than the risks, constraints, or uncertainties. Sure, all of that other stuff needs to come up eventually in the conversation, but bring it in too early and romance goes out the window. (Hi, let me introduce myself. I tend to be neurotic and dependent, and my track record for execution is not good—but I'm working on it . . . .)

We also know that chemistry matters. Look for the sparks, the passion. If your pulse doesn't quicken at any point in the conversation, something is wrong. (Let's face it, most strategy conversations are about as exciting as a night out with Charles and Camilla.)

And progress usually comes over a series of interactions—it's a dance, not a one-act play. Expecting love at first sight just sets you up for disappointment. Pushing too hard too soon sets you up for failure. Patience is key. People who do it best learn to enjoy the chase itself.

Finally, control is an illusion. By definition, the process is edgy and uncomfortable for most of us. There's often a sense of a slippery slope leading to somewhere you're not at all sure that you're ready to go—but when it finally all "clicks" and the pieces fall into place, it all seems so real and so true.

PS: And a good sense of humor really helps get you through the most awkward moments!

STRATEGY IS CULTURE IS STRATEGY
BY KARL E. WEICK

Now here is an interesting thought: that cultures and strategies may be substitutable, and perform remarkably similar functions. They can even be almost identical. Imagine if Karl Weick devoted his ample imagination to missions, visions, goals, objectives, tactics . . . .

> *Culture is a blank space, a highly respected, empty pigeonhole. Economists call it "tastes" and leave it severely alone. Most philosophers ignore it—to their own loss. Marxists treat it obliquely as ideology or superstructure. Psychologists avoid it, by concentrating on child subjects. Historians bend it any way they like. Most believe it matters, especially travel agents. (Douglas, 1982: 183)*

Listed below are four statements extracted verbatim from published articles. The first word in each statement has been deleted. The reader is asked to decide whether the first word in each statement should be *strategy* or *culture*.

> _____ evolves from inside the organization—not from its future environment.

> _____ is a deeply ingrained and continuing pattern of management behavior that gives direction to the organization—not a manipulable and controllable mechanism that can be easily changed from one year to the next.

> _____ is a nonrational concept stemming from the informal values, traditions, and norms of behavior held by the firm's managers and employees—not a rational, formal, logical, conscious, and predetermined thought process engaged in by top executives.

> _____ emerges out of the cumulative effect of many informed actions and decisions taken daily and over years by many employees—not a "one-shot" statement developed exclusively by top management for distribution to the organization . . . .

What I find striking is the plausibility of either term in each sentence. It is as if there were a common set of issues in organizations that some of us choose to call culture and others choose to call strategy. Consider two definitions of culture that I have paraphrased from Douglas (1982) and Keesing (1974):

1.   Culture consists of internally consistent patterns of affirmations, restrictions, and permissions that guide people to behave in sanctioned ways, and that enable people to judge others and justify themselves to others.

2.   Culture consists of a person's theory of what his fellows know, believe, and mean, a theory of what code they are following. It is this theory to which the actor refers when interpreting the unfamiliar and creating sensible events.

With those two definitions in mind, now consider Burgelman's (1983: 66–67) description of corporate strategy:

The concept of corporate strategy represents the more or less explicit articulation of the firm's theory about its past concrete achievements. This theory defines the identity of the firm at any moment in time. It provides a basis for the maintenance of this identity and for the continuity in strategic activity. It induces further strategic initiative in line with it. Corporate-level managers in large, diversified major firms tend to rise through the ranks, having earned their reputation as head of one or more of the operating divisions. By the time they reach the top management level they have developed a highly reliable frame of reference to evaluate business strategies and resource allocation proposals pertaining to the business of the corporation. Top managers, basically, are strategies-in-action whose fundamental strategic premises are unlikely to change.

Common properties shared by the referents of these three definitions are as follows:

1. Their objects are theories rather than facts.
2. They guide both expression and interpretation.
3. They are retrospective, summarizing patterns in past decisions and actions.
4. They are embodied in actions of judging, creating, justifying, affirming, and sanctioning.
5. They summarize past achievements and practices that work.
6. They provide continuity, identity, and a consistent way of ordering the world (i.e., they resemble a code or cosmology).
7. They are social, summarizing what is necessary to mesh one's own actions with those of others.
8. They are often neither completely explicit nor completely articulated, which means that expressions of culture and strategy may vary in specifics.
9. Their substance is seen most clearly when people confront unfamiliar situations where the routine application of existing understanding is not possible.

10. They are tenacious understandings that resist change and that are unlikely to change.

Given these points of correspondence, several implications follow. First, strategy and culture may be substitutable for one another.

> *If values, beliefs, and exemplars are widely shared . . . a well developed organizational culture directs and coordinates activities. By contrast, if an organization is characterized by many different and conflicting values, beliefs, and exemplars, [leaders] cannot expect that their preferences for action will be carried out voluntarily and automatically. Instead, considerable direction and coordination will be required [in the form of] plans, procedures, programs, budgets, and so on [Bresser and Bishop, 1983: 590–591].*

If beliefs, values, and exemplars diverge and become more idiosyncratic, there is a greater necessity for detailed planning. But there is also a greater probability that the detailed plans will not be implemented as intended, because they will be interpreted in diverse ways and lead to divergent actions. Thus the substitutability of culture for strategic plans may be asymmetrical. Culture can substitute for plans more effectively than plans can substitute for culture.

Second, there is the intriguing question of whether strategy is an outgrowth of culture, or vice versa. High-tech companies that start as spinoffs manned by a handful of like-minded people may gain their initial coherence either from shared culture or from shared strategy. Shared strategies usually consist of agreements on means (here's what we can do better than others), whereas shared cultures consist of agreements on ends (here's what we believe more fervently than others). Each form of sharing can represent a fundamentally different starting point for new organizations, with different implications for adaptation and adaptability . . . .

     A third implication of the apparent similarity between culture and strategy is that both may serve a common function. That function is imposing coherence, order, and meaning . . . a fourth implication is that this very coherence may be a liability. A coherent statement of who we are makes it harder for us to become something else. Strong cultures are tenacious cultures. Because a tenacious culture can be a rigid culture that is slow to detect changes in opportunities and slow to change once opportunities are sensed, strong cultures can be backward, conservative instruments of adaptation.

Source: From the article originally titled "The Significance of Corporate Culture" by Karl Weick in Peter J. Frost et al., *Organizational Culture*, pp. 381–389, copyright by Sage Publications. Reprinted by permission of Sage Publications, Inc.

References

Bresser, R. K. and Bishop, R. C. (1983) "Dysfunctional Effects of Formal Planning: Two Theoretical Explanations," *Academy of Management Review*, 8, 1983, pp. 588–599.

Burgelman, R. A. (1983) "A Model of the Interaction of Strategic Behavior, Corporate Context, and the Concept of Strategy," *Academy of Management* Review, 8, pp. 61–70.

Douglas, M. (1982) "Cultural Bias" in *In the Active Voice*, London: Routledge and Kegan Paul, pp. 183–254.

Keesing, R. M. (1974) "Theories of Culture," *Annual Review of Anthropology*, 3, 1974, pp. 73–97.

FIVE EASY STEPS TO DESTROYING A RICH CULTURE (ANY ONE WILL DO)
BY HENRY MINTZBERG

Karl Weick claimed in the last byte that cultures are difficult to change. (Elsewhere he has said the reason is that organizations don't have culture; they *are* cultures.) But Henry, in this byte, begs to disagree. In one sense, they are surprisingly easy to change:

Step 1.   Manage the bottom line (as if you make money by managing money).

Step 2.   Make a plan for every action; no spontaneity please, no learning.

Step 3.   Move managers around so they never get to know anything but management well (and kick the boss upstairs—better to manage a portfolio than a real business).

Step 4.   Always be objective, which means treating people as objects. (In particular, hire and fire employees the way you buy and sell machines—everything is a "portfolio," every human being a human resource.)

Step 5.   Do everything in five easy steps.

HOW DESTRUCTIVE CULTURES DEVELOP
BY TOMMY WISEMAN

In this byte, we find out how destructive cultures develop—much like constructive cultures, in fact, just for the wrong reason—and how they perpetuate themselves. If Karl Weick found culture and strategy to be so close, think here about the relationship between culture and politics. Not so far apart really; they reinforce each other, in a sense. A nice way to end this yin and yang about culture and politics.

Start with a cage containing five monkeys. Inside the cage, hang a banana on a string and place a set of stairs under it. Before long, a monkey will go to the stairs and start to climb toward the banana. As soon as he touches the stairs, spray all of the other monkeys with cold water. After a while, another monkey makes an attempt with the same result, all the other monkeys are sprayed with cold water. Pretty soon, when another monkey tries to climb the stairs, the other monkeys will try to prevent it.

Now, put away the cold water. Remove one monkey from the cage and replace it with a new one. The new monkey sees the banana and wants to climb the stairs. To his surprise and horror, all the other monkeys attack him. After another attempt and attack, he knows that if he tries to climb the stairs he will be assaulted.

Next, remove another of the original five monkeys and replace it with a new one. The newcomer goes to the stairs and is attacked. The previous newcomer takes part in the punishment with enthusiasm! Likewise, replace a third original monkey with a new one, then a fourth, then the fifth. Every time the newest monkey takes to the stairs, he is attacked. By this point, all the monkeys that are beating him have no idea why they were not permitted to climb the stairs or why they are participating in the beating of the newest monkey. After replacing all the original monkeys, none of the remaining monkeys have ever been sprayed with cold water. Nevertheless, no monkey ever again approaches the stairs to try for the banana.

Why not?

Because as far as they know that's the way it's always been done around here. And that, my friends, is how company policy begins.

CHAPTER 9
FINAL FOOD FOR THOUGHT

"Seek simplicity and distrust it."
(Alfred North Whitehead)

"It is better to know some of the questions than all of the answers."
(James Thurber)

"The fox knows many things but the hedgehog knows one big thing."
(Achilochas, circa 650 B.C.)

"There are many paths to the top of the mountain, but the view is always the same."
(Chinese proverb)

"I don't know where you get all these Chinese proverbs."
(Chinese student)

INTRODUCTION TO CHAPTER 9

At this point, tradition has it, we are supposed to
pull all this together, to reveal the magic answer that
will solve all your strategy problems. If you believe
this, you must have been reading another book. This
one has already made its point, namely that strategy
is as follows:

> The little black dress and the emperor's new clothes
> SWOT and magic
> Toilet nirvana
> Cash cows and clever bees
> Art, craft, science
> Einee, meenie, minie, mo
> And lots more
> And lots less

Creating strategy is judgmental designing, intuitive
visioning, and emergent learning; it requires personal
thinking and social interacting, cooperative as well as
conflictive; it can include analyzing before and
programming after as well as imagining during.

Providing any answer short of this would
be doing you a disservice because when it comes to
strategy there are no easy answers. Except, of course,
to make sure you understand deeply what you are

strategizing about, that you act engagingly, responsively, and responsibly, and that you have the courage to see with your own eyes, think with your own brain, and act with your own heart.

Encouraging that has been the purpose of publishing this collection of ideas.

BE YOUR BODY'S BOSS
BY LUCY KELLAWAY

We began this book with a delightful bite from Lucy Kellaway that had nothing—and everything—to do with strategy. So why not almost end with a delectable bite from her that also has nothing and everything to do with strategy.

Which is hardest: to lose weight or to make money? You may think the question is badly put—it is not so much comparing apples with oranges as comparing apples with briefcases.

The reason I ask is because I have been reading a new diet book, *The Business Plan for the Body*, which received a rapturous response in the United States last year and has just been published in Britain.

The concept is that dieting is best approached as an activity roughly like running a business. Each of us, the book states, is CEO of our own body. And every CEO needs a plan—Bill Gates needed a business plan to build Microsoft, and we need one to lose weight. Step one is to come up with a dieting mission statement. Jim Karas, author, MBA and personal trainer, is strict about this. It must say "I am in the weight-loss business" followed by a target for how much weight is to be lost.

Once you have your mission, the next step is a public share offering. You need to go public with your new business. You give presentations and go on a roadshow telling everyone what you are going to do. That done, you set up meetings with your "management team"—friends, spouse, children, colleagues, and boss, and get them on board.

Underlying your dietary business plan is one basic equation. Revenue is food eaten, expenses are calories used up, profit is weight loss.

Investment is exercise and capital is muscle. You crunch through your numbers and watch the pounds roll away. And if you find any of this too hard, Mr. Karas will come in as a management consultant—at a cost of $10,000 a week.

Starting from the top, I'm not sure about the idea of being CEO of my own body. This is either a tautology or nonsense. Even as a metaphor I don't like it. If I am my body's CEO, who is the chairman? Who are the shareholders? If I am CEO, then my body parts must be my employees. In that case, I should be able to fire the lot of them and hire some more comely ones instead.

A dieting mission statement has a stronger parallel with its corporate counterpart, though this is nothing to get excited about. Diet missions are all the same but so too are most company ones—delighting customers, delivering exceptional returns to all stakeholders, and so on. Just as most companies' missions do not help them make money, stating the dieters' aim is not likely to help them get thinner.

As for the roadshows, I admit there is some point in telling people you are dieting, as it makes it harder for you to wolf down a cream doughnut in public. However, there is a style issue here: My relationships with people are founded on the basis that I do not call meetings to spell out changes in my eating habits.

The mathematical formula also bothers me. The basic principle of business is that you try to maximise revenue and minimise costs. Dieting is surely the other way around—you try to minimise the eating and maximise the running around.

You might say that I am being too literal; too British. U.S. readers on Amazon are more tolerant: "Food is 'revenue.'"

Weight loss is 'profit.' Somehow this made sense to me in a way it never had before!" exclaimed one reviewer.

It puzzles me how something as conceptually simple as dieting can be made easier to grasp by reference to business, which is more complex. One can only assume that dieting books have become so far-fetched and full of pseudo-science that this one is simpler by contrast.

Indeed this book shows the dieting genre to be in trouble. I used to think business books were the lowest of the low creatively, always having to borrow other subjects' clothing to look more appealing. There have been books on business as sport, business as acting, as Shakespeare, as war, as the Bible. The barrel is now empty but still writers are scraping. *Marketing Judo* and *Grass Roots Management* are among the latest, outlining respectively what martial arts and lawn maintenance have to teach us about business.

The Business Plan for the Body has reversed this process. Here is a subject so tired that it has turned to business to make it look, dare one say it, fatter.

None of which answers the starting question: which is harder—dieting or making money?

To lose weight all you need do is to stop eating so much and get off the sofa more. It is a solitary pursuit—involving just one person who does the eating and the sitting, and who has only himself to blame if being in the weight loss business does not work out for him.

Making money is surely harder. You need a good idea. You need to be in the right market at the right time. You need to work hard and inspire the people who work for you to do the same. You are dependent on the economy, on luck, and on your own skills and those of others.

So dieting is easier, right?

Wrong. Both are hard, and at both endeavors far more fail than succeed. Yet if the people I know are anything to go by, dieting is tougher: There are a few who have managed to be successful in business but almost none who have lost a few pounds without rediscovering them soon after.

I don't understand why this is so. But I do understand that Mr. Karas has created a great business for himself. Unemployed management consultants, take note.

Source: *Financial Times*, January 13, 2003, London Edition 1, p. 9.

RECIPES FOR COOKING STRATEGY

Finally, if you think we are going to end this book with some sort of recipe for creating strategy, then you are wrong. We are going to end it with two.

Strategy soufflé
"Preheat market expectations to 500 degrees and butter up your outside auditors and directors. Bring profits to boil, remove and place on back burner. Melt down expenses over low heat. Add special financing, shred vigorously. Gradually whisk in fluffed revenue until it doubles in size, increasing heat to your analyst's satisfaction. Transfer mixture to prepared dish and bake until puffed and top is gold. While rising, call your broker and savor before soufflé collapses. Makes 3,800,000,000 helpings."

For the love of strategy
"A recipe is not meant to be followed exactly—it is a canvas on which you can embroider. Add a zest to this, a drop or two of that, a tiny pinch of the other. Let yourself be led by your palate and your tongue, your eyes and your heart. In other words, be guided by your love of food, and then you will be able to cook."

(Chef Roger Vergé)

INDEX